Praise

'Justin has the experience, en͟ and inspiration to
help you sell with passion an͟ purpose, not just in
business but in life. This book is filled with insights
that you can use in every situation.'
— Joseph Clough, #1 bestselling author of
   Be Your Potential, international speaker,
   celebrity coach and hypnotherapist

'Ultimately, this is a book that will appeal not only
to salespeople, but to anybody who is in a position
of management or influence. Whether you're a
seasoned sales professional or just starting out in
your sales journey, there's some great insight here,
but for me, more important were the explanations of
the methods' respective roles in the process. While
some techniques may sound obvious, it's amazing
how many people don't realise their importance, fail
to adopt them and then wonder why they fail. This
book demystifies the process. I'll be keeping my eye
on the bestsellers section.'
— Jon Stump, CEO, Mick George Ltd; *Sunday
   Times* Top Track 250 2018; London Stock
   Exchange Top 1000 Companies to Inspire
   Britain 2017; CIWM Fast 50 Award 2016

'Justin Leigh's *Inspire, Influence, Sell* is a terrific book for anyone in sales or sales management, or those interested in learning more about the psychology and systems involved in developing a strong sales function. It's also a must-read for business owners. The combination of personal stories from Justin's own experience, his INSPIRe sales system, which is explained clearly and thoroughly in the second half of the book, and the many downloadable tools and worksheets make this an excellent reference guide. I particularly like the fact that building relationships is at the heart of the INSPIRe system. People buy from people. Too many sales books gloss over this in favour of the system or process.'

— David B Horne, award-winning author of
Add Then Multiply

'*Inspire, Influence, Sell* is a compelling read. I picked it up at the weekend and couldn't put it down. It's packed with amazing stories and simple, direct insights into what makes a great salesperson. It is one of the best books on the sales process I've ever read, addressing beliefs, skills set and systems. A must-read for anyone who wants to smash it in the world of sales.'

— Arif Anis, bestselling author of
I'MPOSSIBLE, Follow Your Dreams and *Made in Crises*

'This book provides some wonderful insights and practical tips on how to enhance your professionalism and skills as a salesperson. What makes it special is that it also addresses ways to maintain your energy and emotional health, so that you are able to flourish and give your best – especially important for sales and business professionals.'

— Geoff McDonald, cofounder, Minds@work; keynote speaker; mental health campaigner

'What I love about Justin's approach and the INSPIRe methodology outlined in this book is its practicality and the way it can be applied to influence any relationship, not just in selling to customers. Ultimately, *Inspire, Influence, Sell* shows how you can bring your personality and truth to achieve better results for your customers, combined with your passion to deliver value, so you can truly love your roles in sales. If you're in sales or business development, I recommend you read this book.'

— Roei Haberman, Senior Vice President Sales Transformation and Head of TMT, NTT DATA UK

INSPIRE
INFLUENCE
SELL

Master the psychology, skills and systems
of the world's best sales teams

JUSTIN LEIGH

Rᵉthink

First published in Great Britain in 2020 by
Rethink Press (www.rethinkpress.com)

© Copyright Justin Leigh

Cover image © Shutterstock | VectorKnight

Contents

Introduction

If you're in sales, this is the book for you. If you're new to the field, it will be a revelation. If you're established, it will reinforce your belief in what you do and give you a different perspective on how to further improve your performance. Whatever field you're in, you need to be able to sell – it's a fact. At some point in life, you will need to sell yourself, your ideas, your products, your business, your team, your products or services, or your opinion. You continually have to influence and persuade people. That is true for all of us. This book will show you how you can do that while engaging more deeply with the people around you. It will be beneficial to everyone in your life.

If you've bought this book because you want to become a more highly skilled salesperson, I commend you and thank you. This is a valuable investment in yourself, and one that will have a significant impact on your future – but only if you read, understand and apply what you learn. If you follow the instructions and the system, answer the questions, try the exercises and apply what you're learning, you'll become a highly successful salesperson. What you learn in this book will also strengthen your relationships with your family, partner, children, friends, colleagues and clients. It will help you understand the people around you. It will stimulate your thinking and allow you to achieve things you never thought possible. It will help you attract opportunities for growth, development and, ultimately, success.

I hope your interest is piqued and that you're excited. You should be! Whatever your current circumstances, whatever your ambitions, get ready for a step change in your abilities and the most incredible future you can imagine.

Before we start, let's do a reality check. A lot of people absolutely detest salespeople. They consider them to be slimy, smarmy, pushy, overzealous, loud, crass, cocky, obnoxious and full of themselves. If you're a salesperson (as I was), you may have encountered people who have this view. And if you've worked as part of a large sales organisation that doesn't train its salespeople, you may even understand why some people have this opinion. The truth is, there are a lot of bad salespeople out there. Now when I say 'bad salespeople', I mean lazy or untrained salespeople – salespeople who have either, a) never been trained in their role, or b) never taken the time to learn how to sell properly. While it might seem difficult and time-consuming to learn to sell 'the right way', selling more effectively would significantly benefit them and their clients.

I have learned throughout my career that for sales-people to be successful we must focus on three vital areas: psychology, skills and systems. Psychology is the foundation of success in sales and will determine whether or not we believe we are able to succeed. Without belief, we cannot convince ourselves that we are capable of success. We will continually revisit principles of psychology throughout this book.

Selling is a learned skill and can be taught to any-one who is willing to learn and *change* the way that they work. I cannot emphasise enough the need for change. The world is changing rapidly. Your clients (and their clients) and their needs are changing al-most constantly. The only way you can continue to be relevant to your clients is by changing the way you work. You must continually improve yourself so that you can meet their future requirements. In this book, I'll share with you a tried, tested and trusted way to improve your sales capability, so that you'll become the best salesperson you're able to be, and in turn, surpass your clients' needs, now and in the future.

Selling is serving

Some people have a hard time shaking the negative connotation that comes with a position in sales, or even the thought of selling. But if you consider selling to be serving, you'll think differently about sales. You're helping your clients get everything they need, and you're ensuring they choose you to provide it for them. This shift in thinking can be liberating if you have any reservations about what selling 'should be'. You should be establishing a foundation that is ethical, honest and about serving your client – this is what separates 'the best in the market' from 'the rest of the market'.

This book will introduce you to the INSPIRe Secret Sales System, a simple, powerful and effective system that will imprint on your unconscious mind so that you won't have to concentrate on remembering it. This system will naturally become your preferred sales methodology. Throughout the book, you'll see specific references to the INSPIRe Secret Sales System as well as more general references to the sales process. This is intentional. It acknowledges the importance of structure and processes when it comes to successful selling, whether through the INSPIRe Secret Sales System or a similar sales process.

We'll also address motivation, the importance of changing behaviours and habits, and how to sustain improvements over the long term. If you're interested in quick fixes or wins, or just selling more, you'll see moderate improvement as a result of working through this book, but I ask you to dig deeper. Join me on the voyage of discovery and make a commitment to 'master your art' over the long term. The content of this book was born out of a passion for learning about success, high performance and personal transformation.

The INSPIRe Secret Sales System came about through my own search for the most effective sales methodology. I spent years tailoring the techniques and principles of other sales programmes because I couldn't find one that was simple enough to use consistently (without multiple aids and prompts) but comprehensive enough to make a real impact. I've amalgamated my skills and experience across sales, strategic account management, leadership, business strategy, coaching and NLP (neuro-linguistic programming) to create this sales manual and the accompanying training that I deliver to organisations. With a career history that spans over twenty-five years and many disciplines, I am in the unique position of being able to offer this sales success model.

If you haven't read *The Greatest Salesman in the World*, by Og Mandino,[1] I highly recommend it. This iconic book explains what it takes to become successful salespeople. While Mandino's book teaches people

---

1   O Mandino, *The Greatest Salesman in the World* (Jaico Publishing House, 2008)

about the what, this book teaches you about the how – specifically, what are the steps you should follow? What is the 'recipe' for sales success? If you're working hard in sales but not reaping the results you know you should be, then working harder isn't the answer. Changing your approach using a tried and tested method, combined with hard work, will put you on the road to success. I advise you not just to read but to 'work through' this book. There are many opportunities to reflect and take action in ways that will support your development and strengthen your ability to inspire, influence and sell.

Whether you're new to sales, an experienced sales professional or a leader looking to improve the consistency and performance of your sales organisation, you'll gain immense value from this book. It lays out a memorable sales process over several chapters and also includes mastery content for each stage of the system, which will give you deeper insight and expertise. The combination of foundational and specialist material ensures that no matter where you're starting from, you can become a skilled salesperson. You might want to work through this book at the foundational level for each chapter and return to the Sales Mastery sections once you get to grips with the overall system and have developed your skills. Each chapter starts with an experience story in which I share relevant, valuable and sometimes funny anecdotes. If you prefer to dive straight into the sales system, you can skip that content. This book is designed to be accessible and flexible, so that you get the most out of it.

As you work through each chapter, I suggest you make notes in a journal or notebook. This will help you learn and adopt the content.

Let's start *our* journey together and *your* extraordinary transformation.

PART ONE

PREPARATION

1

Selling: The Fundamentals

When I first became a sales representative, in 1994, I worked for a medium-sized company based in Dundee, Scotland. It was a company that sold dental products to dentists, and I had previously worked as a dental technician. I remember how nervous I was starting at a new, larger company (the dental laboratory had four staff, and this company employed about 500). I had no experience in sales and knew little about the way dental practices used and ordered products.

I spent just one week in training at the Dundee head office, where I was introduced to the key people in the organisation and trained on the products the company manufactured. I also spent two days in the field with members of their senior sales team covering different parts of Scotland. At the end of that first week, I was given the keys to my company car, a selection of the Yellow Pages that corresponded with my sales territory, a box of record cards and a fax machine. I was allowed to leave early (at 4.30pm) on the Friday afternoon so that I could make the seven-and-a-half-hour drive home from Dundee. I got home late but still feeling a buzz about the exciting journey I was starting. I spent the weekend thumbing through the dental practices in the Yellow Pages, making my record cards and planning my journey for the first week on my new sales territory (previously vacant and unmanaged).

It was a true voyage of discovery. I worked for that company for almost two years and was fairly success-ful – *without ever being taught how to sell*. It wasn't until I moved to the next company that I was put through a formal sales training programme with the company's sales trainer. The programme was comprehensive but complex, and remembering all the elements of the training was difficult. But once I'd grasped the fun-damentals of the model and practised selling, my confidence with clients and, more importantly, my results improved dramatically. I took what I'd learned and applied it to my client meetings, and the differ-ence it made in my ability to meet my clients' needs, and win more business as a result, *when I got it right*, was revolutionary.

Become client-centred in your approach

To sell (or serve) effectively, you must focus on your client – even if it creates more work for you. This is a fundamental principle of sales. Committing to meeting the needs of your client gives you a huge competitive advantage. It also has many positive side-effects.

- Your mindset will shift to one of service towards your clients.

- You will unconsciously communicate a deeper level of commitment to your clients.

- Any pressure you feel to 'make the sale' will be reduced.

- You'll foster stronger, more meaningful relationships.

- You'll create authentic, genuine propositions that truly meet your clients' needs.

If you start from this position and remind yourself (and your teams) that the most important perspective is always that of the client, the experience you create will mean so much more for your clients.

At every stage of interaction with your clients, ask yourself, 'If I look at this ONLY from my client's perspective, how does it need to be?'

This reframing of your point of view will put you among the best salespeople on the planet!

Ten staggering sales statistics

The Brevet Group published a blog post titled '21 mind-blowing sales stats'.[2] Here is my interpretation of ten of their most relevant findings:

- There are 21 million people working in sales and 55% of them don't have the necessary skills to succeed.

- Fewer than 15% of customers surveyed agreed that a salesperson could understand what they need.

- Nine out of ten customers claim they would give referrals, yet just one in ten salespeople actually ask.

- The salespeople who do ask for referrals can earn almost five times more than those who don't.

- Eight out of ten sales need five follow-up calls after a customer meeting, yet more than 40% of salespeople stop after just one.

- Over 90% of customer sales contact happens over the phone.

---

2   B Williams, '21 Mind-Blowing Sales Stats' (Brevet, no date), https://blog.thebrevetgroup.com/21-mind-blowing-sales-stats, accessed 9 September 2020

- It takes eight cold calls to reach a new potential customer.

- Almost eight out of ten salespeople who use social media to sell outperform their peers.

- The investment in ongoing sales training can increase net sales per employee by as much as 50%.

- When you measure recall following a presentation, 63% of people remember stories but a mere 5% of people can remember statistics.

Process or personality?

There's a common misperception that selling is only about relationships and the salesperson's personality. While having personality and being able to build relationships is helpful in sales, knowing how to sell will trump relationships and personality every single time. I've seen this over and over in my career as a salesperson, sales leader/coach and sales trainer. In fact, my experience has shown me that reliance on relationships and personality, to the detriment of the sales process, can negatively affect the salesperson's performance. For example, I've seen salespeople get invited to clients' weddings or special events, while at the same time, they slowly lose business from those clients.

Not everyone is born with an outgoing, strong and positive personality, but you can develop your relationship skills, or 'rapport development' skills, over time. So don't be concerned if you feel that your personality isn't 'big enough' – I certainly worried about that in the past too. Once you learn the INSPIRe Secret Sales System and the fundamentals of rapport development, you'll have the keys to a successful future as a sales professional.

It's also true that once you utilise a sales process and begin to realise results from it, the increase in your ability and confidence can be staggering. This in turn strengthens your client relationships and helps you develop your own 'sales personality'. Your starting point is simply sales structure rather than personality. If the reverse is true, and you have personality already and start to use the process effectively, you'll be unstoppable!

My ten commandments of sales

These commandments, combined with a sales structure, show what it takes to be successful in sales and business. I teach them to all my clients.

1. Focus entirely on your client

2. Use a value-led approach

3. Tap into your intense passion

4. Continuously develop your expertise

5. Be exceptionally curious

6. Listen intently and create space

7. Enjoy the process and the results

8. Believe in your solution and yourself

9. Persevere until you succeed

10. Get to 'yes' or 'no'

I won't expand on these here, but throughout the book we'll look at them in the systems, stories and principles we cover.

Three important components of your client proposition

Your clients will be assessing:

1. **You, the salesperson:**
   - Can you be trusted?
   - Will you deliver what they need?
   - Are you knowledgeable, credible, engaged and likeable?

2. **Your product or service:**
   - Does your product or service do what they need it to do?

- What is different or unique about it?
- Is it a brand they recognise or trust?

3. **Your organisation:**

   - Is your company reputable?
   - What is the feedback from other clients?
   - What are the independent ratings of the service provided?
   - How well does it deal with issues, complaints or refunds?

Your client is looking to see if you, your product and your organisation can be trusted to deliver what they need and if these things 'fit' their business – they may not do this consciously, but they will do so intuitively. We'll cover how this fits within the sales process, but at this stage, it's important to consider how you consistently represent yourself, your product and your organisation to give your client confidence in these three priority areas. A gap in any one of these areas will create doubt for your client and jeopardise your chances of success.

Your personal vision

As you work through this sales manual, you'll learn many principles and practices that will help you hone your sales skills. You'll set yourself personal goals. I also recommend that you create a personal vision of the salesperson you wish to become. As an executive coach, I've worked with business leaders to clarify the visions they set for themselves and their organisations. While there are many different types of visions, two have stood out to me:

- Provide world-class service to my clients
- Be the most trusted and respected supplier to my clients

Imagine if you made it your intention to be both 'world-class' and 'the most trusted and respected supplier' to your clients. It would force a new level of thinking about how you operate. This is an incredibly high aspiration. I hope that when you consider this for yourself, you feel a mixture of emotions, as I do: a little fear, some scepticism, increasing curiosity and a swelling of excitement. Keep in mind that the achievements of every successful person, product and organisation were once no more than aspirations. This is where you are right now. If you identify your own personal vision and start 'living it' from this day forward, you'll be setting a course for an astronomical breakthrough with your clients.

I hope this discussion is already stimulating thoughts and ideas. Let's get started with the reflection. Take a moment now to write about your personal vision in your journal or notebook.

- What will inspire you to become the best sales professional possible?

- What do you want your clients to experience when they choose to work with you?

You may also want to consider other points covered in this chapter and write about them. What are your thoughts and some possible actions you can take?

2

The Power Of Change

In recent roles leading business teams in organisations, I was approached to act as an adviser, or mentor, to people within the organisation who wanted advice on how to 'get on' in the company. While each person had different needs, skills, experiences and ambitions, similar themes emerged. In these discussions, the key point I emphasised was that without the openness, willingness and desire to change, you cannot develop, improve and achieve your future goals.

The ability to change is everything.

Once the person and I had established and agreed on the importance of change, the conversation would focus on three simple but powerful ideas:

- Commit to mastery and decide on a future role

- Gain future role experience immediately

- Set goals and take consistent action towards them

Let's look at each more closely.

Commit to mastery and decide on a future role

First, you must commit to becoming the best you're capable of being in your current role. Become the go-to person – someone who is known to be an expert and who consistently delivers their best over the long term. No spotty performance, no slacking – always delivering and searching for ways to improve and stay at the top. Second, you must be clear on what you want your future role to be. For some, this might involve a promotion. In the right company, performing at your best gets you recognition and promotions. I appreciate there are exceptions to this, but it's worth remembering that even if this isn't true for your organisation, there is no downside to this approach. If you're focused on development, you'll become so valuable that you can move on elsewhere, if not within your own organisation. What's important is to define the future role. This will give you a point of focus – a target to aim for.

Gain future role experience immediately

I learned early in my career that it's difficult to be ready for your next role if you don't have experience doing it in some way. There is immense value in gaining experience in advance. It pushes you outside of your comfort zone, forces you to learn new skills, adds value to your business and prepares you for the future. There may be some pressure involved in the learning process, but this is fantastic preparation and life experience. It will make you a more well-rounded, confident person. Once you're clear on your next role, speak with your line manager and peers about your aspirations. They can help you find opportunities to 'step up' and develop. Most people wait for a promotion and then get frustrated when they're overlooked, even though they haven't done anything tangible to prepare themselves. Don't wait for the promotion to get the experience. Take action. One other thing to consider – don't get hung up on being paid more or getting rewarded for taking on additional responsibilities. The money and rewards will come when you have the experience and are able to move upwards to that role. For now, appreciate the opportunity to develop yourself. Once you've learned a skill or gained experience, it is yours to keep. It becomes part of you, and that is priceless.

Set goals and take consistent action towards them

Once you're motivated to change, you're committed to being the best you can be, and you know what you want, set your goals and clarify the actions you'll take towards them. Setting and achieving goals is what separates high performers from the rest of the population. Make a habit of setting goals and taking action and it will pay you back tenfold over time. A number of goal-setting templates allow you to document and track your performance against your goals, including apps that you can use on your mobile, tablet or PC. Here's an example: https://bit.ly/Reach-your-goals.

Goal-setting fundamentals

When setting goals, it's important to use positive statements, ie, be clear about what you want rather than what you don't want. While this advice may be overused, it cannot be overemphasised. Our minds cannot process negative goals. The unconscious mind will work to achieve whatever you put your focus and attention on. While you can use consequences to spur you into action, you must not let them be the defined goal. Clearly state your goals (and write them down whenever possible) so that you give your mind (and your actions) a target. Consider these statements:

- I really don't want to miss my sales targets this year.

- I'm going to over-deliver by 10% against my sales target this year.

The second statement is much more effective. Even if you don't achieve the 10% growth over your target figure, your mind, your plan and your actions are firmly centred on overachievement. Repeatedly asking yourself how you will achieve the 10% over target will stimulate thoughts and actions that will drive you to greater success. Be conscious of the goals you set for yourself, and make sure you use positive statements when writing them down. This simple principle will revolutionise your results.

Your career journey

In my working life so far, I've had twelve different careers (including being an author/speaker/executive coach). While this number might sound high, it falls within an average. According to the Bureau of Labor Statistics, the average US worker will have 12.3 jobs in their working lifetime, and that number is rising. Workers now stay, on average, just four years in a role or an organisation.[3] While companies are trying

---

3 'Number of jobs, labor market experience, and earnings growth: Results from a national longitudinal survey' [news release] (US Department of Labor Bureau of Labor Statistics, 2019), www.bls.gov/news.release/pdf/nlsoy.pdf, accessed 28 September 2020

to figure out how they can keep employees loyal, employees are focusing on increasing their value so they're ready for change when the time is right.

The best way to prepare yourself is to acquire skills and experience that can be easily transferred – skills and experience that will be valuable in the future as well as now. Once you set your mind to it, you can achieve virtually anything: you just need the time, practice and determination to improve yourself every single day. With this commitment, you can become one of the highest-performing people in your field (or any field). What's more, you'll have a highly valued, transferable skill set.

My career has been a journey with numerous stops and changes along the way. Each part of the journey has formed the foundation for the next and given me a helping hand. As you develop skills and competence in one area, you'll naturally aspire to improve or challenge yourself further. This level of internal desire presents amazing opportunities for personal growth and satisfaction.

Initiating change

Changing our behaviours and habits can take a tremendous amount of effort, but the results are well worth it. Before we can change, we must be aware of and break through our existing blocks, resistance and forgetfulness. The well-documented 'Ebbinghaus Forgetting Curve' describes how we lose memory of learned knowledge over time, with as little as 25% of knowledge retained after just six days. But with action planning, reflection, repetition and coaching, this can be increased to as high as 90%.[4]

Through my client work and career to date, I've learned that to make lasting change, you must envision a powerful and compelling future and then clearly identify your personal motives (your motivation for change), capture them and revisit them regularly. Awareness of your resistance to change and a compelling reason to change will be a source of energy that keeps your motivation levels high. Throughout this book, you'll find opportunities to identify your reasons for change and actions you can take. This will help you gain clarity on your motivation and the ways in which you'll make that change happen.

Taking notes, reflecting on them and then committing to action will fuel your desire to improve and ensure your future success. I recommend making a commitment to yourself in advance – a commitment that evokes a powerful emotional response in you. We'll revisit it often, so you're held accountable to change and can access the best version of you.

---

4   H Ebbinghaus, *Memory: A contribution to experimental psychology* (1885), available from CD Green, 'Classics in the history of psychology' (York University, no date), http://psychclassics.yorku.ca/Ebbinghaus/index.htm, accessed 28 September 2020

Before we move on, reflect on this chapter and write down your thoughts in your journal or notebook.

- What level of performance would you like to reach?

- Why is it important that you embrace change and strengthen your skills?

- How will you keep yourself on track when you're busy or you lose focus?

3

Setting Yourself Up To Win

Imagining a future that holds incredible success can be difficult and a little scary. Depending on your up-bringing, self-image and unconscious programming, it can be stressful to think about a big change, even when that change is positive.

I've faced this challenge several times in my life. Whenever I'm looking to make a significant change, I'm aware that, on an unconscious level, it's going to require a considerable amount of effort. I'm not telling you this to put you off but to get you in the right frame of mind – you need to get momentum and maintain it to make a lasting change. During these times in my life, I've worked through exercises like the one we'll look at now to help me create a clear vision of the fu-ture I want to achieve and to experience it in advance.

This is the best way to connect with and believe in the goal you've created. The exercise below will help you start to make an unconscious shift in mindset.

Visualisation

Done correctly and regularly, visualisation (ie, mental rehearsal) can be a powerful tool to boost your confidence and, in turn, your success. We all visualise a lot of the time but don't always realise it. We also don't always realise how visualisation affects us and that we have the power to control our thoughts. With visualisation, you create the future in advance. And with routine practice and clearly defined outcomes, you can make visualisation an extraordinarily effective force in your life. Try it for yourself and see.

EXERCISE: WHAT DOES THE FUTURE LOOK LIKE?

Take a few minutes to write down in your journal or notebook *why* it's important for you to improve your performance in the future.

To prepare for this exercise, I recommend doing this:

- Take five deep breaths – in and out.
- Think about a time in the future – at least a year from now. Imagine that you have transformed yourself:
    - You are the highest-performing salesperson in your organisation.

- You have made an incredible impact on yourself and the people around you – your clients, family and friends.
- You have become recognised as highly accomplished and successful.
- You have unlocked a high level of skill and experience.
- You have a strong sense of satisfaction, pride and achievement.

Make notes in your journal or notebook.

- What does this look like?
- How does this sound?
- What are you feeling about yourself?

Now that you've experienced what it's like to go through this transformation, let's look at what you will have achieved. This is an opportunity to address key goal-setting areas and gain greater clarity about what success looks like to you.

Consider these areas to set yourself *performance goals* (you don't need to set goals in all these areas, but make sure you've set some in the areas most important to you):

- Finances (earnings, savings, investments)
- Family (your influence and example)
- Career (roles available to you)
- Personal growth and development (skills you have mastered and are working on)
- Freedom (sense of flow and achievement)
- Time (working patterns and personal time)
- Life fulfilment (how you feel about yourself and your life)

- Mastery (being the best you can be)
- Your choice – what else is important to you?

Once you've captured these future performance goals, take a few moments to read through them and really connect with them.

Write down what you notice in your journal or notebook. These goals are going to be important for your motivation to change as we go through this book. They'll keep your engine running, especially when old habits and behaviour patterns try to resurface.

I recommend revisiting this exercise regularly to remind yourself of the change you want to produce in your life. This will keep you focused and motivated. You might want to note this page so you can come back to it.

Before we move on, reflect on this chapter and write down your thoughts in your journal or notebook.

4

Prepare² – Be Ready For Success

Having worked as a sales manager, I know first-hand the importance of comprehensive preparation. Years ago, I had an important client meeting. A member of my team and I were due to meet with, and present to, a number of senior decision makers from a public organisation. The business proposition, the team, the product portfolio and our service offering were all strong, but so was the competition.

To prepare for the presentation, the salesperson met with the client to understand their requirements. This provided us with the insight we needed, and we designed our presentation around meeting their true needs. We were also aware that they wanted to see how committed we were to winning the business and supporting the teams working in the organisation. I had this in mind as I researched the organisation and the board of directors, and I uncovered the CEO's blog. In it, she wrote about a recent challenge due to severe flooding. She recognised the efforts of the teams working in the organisation and their commitment to their own clients and service users. There was a story about a member of staff who had borrowed her father's tractor to overcome the floods and get to work to keep the organisation functioning. I was impressed by the commitment this team member had shown and by the fact that the CEO had recognised it. I took a screen shot of the blog and included it in the presentation.

During the presentation, I referenced the commitment of the clients' team (this team member in particular) and drew a comparison with my team members – who were committed to the client and their service users. Several companies submitted proposals to compete for the business, but our team won. We received excellent feedback, especially in terms of how we demonstrated our commitment. This was due largely to our preparation. Preparation is without a doubt a key to sales success.

The importance of preparation

I know that talk of preparation and planning can seem unnecessary, perhaps even boring. But conditioning yourself to properly prepare will help you perform at your best consistently and put you among the top 10% of the sales population. A common misperception is that good salespeople don't need to prepare – they can 'wing it'. While they may well achieve short-term results, these same people could double or even triple their performance if they invested time in preparation. Give yourself the opportunity to be in the top tier of salespeople.

When you're occupied with a task, you adopt a state of mind without conscious effort or thought. This mental state may or may not be the 'ideal' state of mind with which to engage your clients. You can make a hugely positive impact on your performance simply by getting yourself into an enabling state of mind: one where you have an outlook and attitude that enables you to perform at the highest possible level. Your mindset is a vital component of success.

Revisit your performance goals. Now recognise that you'll achieve them faster if you develop the habit of preparing for each sales interaction with your clients. In your journal or notebook, write 'The reason I need to prepare for each of my sales interactions with clients is…'

Then write down your reason.

Now that we understand why preparation is important, let's look at the Prepare² framework.

The framework

For many people, preparing for customer meetings can feel overwhelming. They don't know where to start, so they don't start. They don't do any preparation and risk being not only ill-prepared but also drastically reducing their chances of success. If you or the team you manage are having low success rates with client meetings – ie the client isn't choosing to work with you or your team – it's likely to be one of two things: poor preparation or a poor sales process.

Some sales teams I led in the past often didn't prepare because they made it seem more complicated and time-consuming than it needed to be. With the right framework, it can be simple and powerful.

Over the years (and through many mistakes and successes), I identified four areas on which attention should be focused when preparing for a client meeting. I call it the Prepare[2] (or 'prepare squared') framework. See the diagram below.

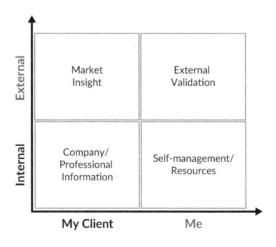

Prepare[2] Framework: The Client Preparation Model

Let's look at each of these areas.

My client

We should always start here. The client is the most important factor in any sales interaction. We must orientate ourselves around them – their business and their perspective. Without the client, there are no sales. There is no growth and no business. It's obvious but often overlooked.

Internal

This is about researching the client and what's happening to them in their business. Consider the following when seeking information about a potential client and their organisation:

- Strategic vision and plans

- Company announcements

- Website and social media channels

- Network and third parties

- Key decision makers

By understanding our potential client and their business, we are stepping into their world. We can be empathetic. Once we know about our client and how we can serve them and create value, we can have more meaningful interactions with them.

A caveat here: don't make too many assumptions. Be informed in advance of a meeting, but still ask questions. Be infinitely curious about the potential client's business and how you can best serve them.

External

This is about understanding what's happening in the client's marketplace and external environment. Consider these areas to gain further insight:

- Future market trends

- Competitive activity

- Market landscape

- Potential opportunities

- Potential threats

Once we understand what's happening externally for our customers, or potential customers, we can start to align our messaging and preparation. We must consider how we might help them navigate these external factors more effectively, now and in the future.

After preparing on behalf of our client, we must prepare ourselves.

Me

Internal

We must make sure that we know our products and/or portfolio. We need to be clear on our value propositions, our points of differentiation, our unique selling points, the benefits that our product or service provides and how we can position these benefits in a way that is meaningful for our client.

Consider these areas when doing internal preparation:

- Personal preparation
- Insights and knowledge
- Relevant experience and examples
- Sales system
- Tools, assets, resources, programs

External

It's critical to think about our business from an external perspective. Many clients will want to see external validation of our work or services, and that external validation must come from independent and objective sources. If it doesn't, it won't seem valid and could actually work against us.

Here are some areas to consider in terms of external preparation:

- Use cases and/or studies
- Results data
- Whole-life cost models/return-on-investment evidence
- Models and systems
- Testimonials, references and referrals

The Prepare^2 framework is a powerful model for preparation. You can download a copy of the template I use to help my clients prepare for every important client meeting here: https://bit.ly/Prepare2-Tool.

By using this template in advance of any significant client meeting, you'll drastically increase your rates of success. Combine this with a proven sales process and you'll be unstoppable!

Sales Mastery: Preparing for success and engaging your client

Personal preparation

To be at your best, you must tap into your most resourceful state of mind. Before an important competition, athletes get themselves into 'the zone' or a state of flow to heighten their performance. You can do the same.

Here's a proven way to create this powerful, positive state of mind. I recommend doing this preparation immediately before every interaction you have with a client. Complete this exercise as a starting point, and then revisit it before each client meeting to create a positive experience for you and your client.

In your journal or notebook, write the answers to these questions:

- Who does your client need you to be in order to choose you?

- What attitude and mindset do you need to adopt to be at your best?

- Think of a time when you were at your best – confident and in the zone. What did you see, hear, feel or say to yourself?

- Imagine the perfect interaction with your client. Both of you are enjoying the discussion, and the client thanks you for supporting them to make the right decision. Capture what you see, hear, feel and say.

Take a few moments to read through your responses. Allow the full potential of this exercise to resonate with you. *Become aware of how excited and positive doing so makes you feel.*

Capture what you notice in your journal or notebook.

The importance of this preparation ritual will become apparent once you start using it as part of your sales practice. You'll be able to consistently bring your best self to your clients. And they *will* notice this and appreciate your intention to be your best self for their benefit. While it takes effort at first, if you prepare this way for every client interaction for the next three weeks, you'll not only realise the benefits but also create a habit that will take over. You'll no longer have to think about doing this. In fact, it will seem easier to prepare than to 'wing it'.

Simply returning to this page and reading your notes will help you to develop this ritual and form a positive habit for the future.

Engaging your potential client

If you're in a field with a longer sales cycle and your role involves pre-arranged client meetings and developing relationships over time, there are important additional considerations when it comes to preparing for meetings.

Regardless of whether you're tasked with engaging your clients or working from leads passed to you from your organisation, the way in which you engage with your clients and manage your meetings with them will be similar.

You must:

- Research your client
- Engage your client (the 'hook')
- Set meeting objectives
- Prepare personally

We're going to work through these in order.

Research your client

We live in a wonderful digital age. People's interests, activities, successes and even failures are likely to be posted somewhere on the internet. With this wealth of information, you would be remiss not to use it in preparation for a client meeting. Here are a few pointers on how to go about conducting research.

Google your client: You may be surprised by what you find. I once found out one of my clients was involved in a charity. Learning this about him gave me a new level of respect for him and also gave us a topic for a discussion that created a stronger relationship.

Check out their social media profiles: If you find your client on Facebook, Instagram, Twitter or LinkedIn, you'll see what they like and share. Which groups are they a member of and who or what are they following and contributing to? You'll also see who they're connected to and which of those connections you have in common. You've probably heard about six degrees of separation? In my experience, it's now closer to two or three.

Review their organisation's website: Look for the organisation's vision, mission and values. If it has a strategic plan, read the headlines and get an understanding of what your client's aspirations may be. Knowing about your client's organisation, whatever their position in it, will help you to create some common ground – critical for building rapport. More on that shortly.

Engage your client (the 'hook')

Now that you know a little about your client from the research that you've completed, you're in a great position to engage them with a strong 'hook'. The hook is a statement (or series of statements) that does one or more of these things:

- Highlights potential common ground between you and the client

- Identifies potential issues the client may have and hints that you might have a solution

- References a relevant connection, interest or mutual acquaintance

- Shares evidence of how your service or organisation is helping clients or the industry

- Asks for a meeting (or call) to discover how you might work together

The hook *should not* be an attempt to sell to your client – it's too early at this stage of the relationship. If you position your hook (either over the phone or in an email) in the right way, conveying only a benefit to your client, your likelihood of getting a positive response is high.

Whether you prefer phone calls or emails, I suggest you try both, in that order. Ask yourself, 'If I received this call or email from a complete stranger, would I respond?' If the answer is no, look at your script and reword it until it's so compelling and focused on you (as the client) that you'd be convinced by it and respond. This will create a template for you to work from – and it will likely be relevant to a number of your clients.

Here's a template you can download and use to guide you in writing your hook: https://bit.ly/Prepare2-Hook.

Set meeting objectives

So, you've engaged your client. Now you need to confirm the meeting and share your suggested objectives for the discussion. Here's a structure I recommend for setting meeting objectives – it will prime the meeting for the sales process:

1. Discuss your client's current and future priorities and challenges.

2. Provide examples of [your organisation's] successful client programmes.

3. Discuss possible solutions and next steps.

This structure will integrate into a standard email template and look something like this, a fictional email to Daniel at Success Trading Ltd:

Dear Daniel,

Many thanks for the confirmation of our meeting next Wednesday, the 20th of June, at the London office of Success Trading at 9.30am.

Here is my suggested agenda for the meeting:

1. Discussion about Success Trading's current (and future) priorities and challenges.

2. Examples of Inspire Ltd's successful client programmes.

3. Discussion about possible solutions and next steps.

I hope this agenda meets your expectations and approval.

I'm happy to discuss other topics during the meeting. If there is anything specific you would like me to prepare or bring with me, please do let me know.

I look forward to seeing you next week and to a productive and inspiring meeting.

Until then.

Kind regards, etc.

Having a format that you know works and that you can use to communicate with your clients in advance of meetings will make you more effective, save you time and deliver more value to the client.

Here's an email template you can use: https://bit.ly/Prepare2-EMail-Template. Play around with the wording until you find a version that works for you.

Prepare personally

To ensure that you go into your client meetings in the best frame of mind and give yourself the optimal chance for success, it's important to prepare yourself on a personal level.

Make sure you have what you need. Necessary items may include some or all of these things:

- Literature folder
- Product catalogue and codes
- Demonstration product
- Samples (where appropriate)

- Case-study documents

- Evidence

- Client testimonials

- References

- Technical data sheets

- Pricing workbooks

- Discount structures

- Distributor details

- Promotional literature

- Notepad and pen

- Business cards

- Laptop/tablet/projector (if relevant)

This may seem obvious to those of you in sales. But the number of times I've been in client meetings with salespeople who realise that they don't have everything they need to hold a meaningful discussion about their company, the product or the service is truly incredible. Always be prepared.

Over the years I've learned that while I don't always like the process of preparation, when I'm fully prepared, my confidence, ability and performance skyrocket. I'm sure you have experienced this yourself. Appreciate the value of preparation – it pays dividends.

EXERCISE: TAKE TIME TO VISUALISE

Below is another simple visualisation script. Read through it to familiarise yourself with it, and then follow the instructions.

Relax and take three deep breaths. When you're ready, close your eyes and imagine this:

1. You're at the end of the meeting with your client.
2. You're both smiling as you shake hands to say goodbye.
3. The meeting has gone better than you expected.
4. The client shared a number of relevant priorities and challenges with you.
5. You understood exactly what your client needed.
6. Your client agreed you were the one who could help.
7. You have agreed on a plan that will help them and deliver the results you want.
8. Notice how good this feels and what you see, hear, experience and say to yourself.

I hope you enjoyed this activity. Remember, when you practise visualisation regularly, it will become a formidable force in your preparation for client meetings.

You're now ready to work through the INSPIRe Secret Sales System. But before we move on, reflect on this chapter and write down your thoughts in your journal or notebook.

PART TWO

LAYING THE FOUNDATION

5

The INSPIRe Secret Sales System

During my many years as a salesperson, key account manager and sales manager, I received training on countless different sales processes and programs. Some of the content was excellent, and I gained useful insights that helped shape my career. One of the challenges I had early in my sales career was managing the process of selling consistently – and I noticed many people in my sales team struggling with this as well when I started as a sales manager. It could be confusing trying to remember what should happen in what order, alongside managing a portfolio, keeping the clients engaged, handling issues and working in sometimes stressful situations.

As W Edwards Deming stated, 'A system must have an aim. Without an aim, there is no system.'[5] The system is important, as it helps with reproducibility and consistency. The aim is just as vital. Understanding both gives us the results we're looking for.

I never attended a programme that conveyed a clear, simple process that also incorporated depth, knowledge and experience. There was always a level of complexity that made the process difficult to adopt. On a number of training workshops, in a number of contexts, I repeatedly heard the acronym KISS (keep it simple stupid) but never felt that it was delivered in any of the sales training models I'd been taught. I was always left wanting. As a leader, the quote above from W Edwards Deming often played on my mind. If the process you want to follow isn't clear, your team simply can't achieve consistent, reproducible results. It's no use looking to people for results if the process isn't clear and useable.

Developing a model

Shortly after I started working as a key account manager and began developing my skills as a people leader, I discovered coaching. In coaching, the GROW model is well recognised. GROW is a simple mnemonic (memory device) that provides the coach with

---

5   W Edwards Deming, *The New Economics for Industry, Government, Education* (Massachusetts Institute of Technology, 1994)

a process that will allow them to be consistent in their approach and effectively deliver the result that both the coach and their client desire. This model is used the world over and is recognised as the framework that underpins many coaches' work with clients. I started to use the model with my team, family and friends and found it remarkable. It works every time.

Here's a summary of the GROW model:

G – Goal   (What is the client's goal?)

R – Reality   (What is the client's current reality?)

O – Options   (What options does the client have?)

W – Will   (What will the client commit to do now?)

This model is so well used that it has been expanded and adapted by various coaching organisations. A recent enhancement is To GROWME, which broadens the scope of the coaching session:

To – Topic   (What is the priority topic of the coaching session?)

G – Goal   (What is the client's goal?)

R – Reality   (What is the client's current reality?)

O – Options   (What options does the client have?)

W – Will   (What will the client commit to do now?)

M – Monitor   (What will the client do to stay on track?)

E – Evaluate   (How will the client know that they've been successful?)

I have successfully used the GROW and To GROWME coaching models (as have thousands of other coaches and leaders) because they are simple and effective. When I started using these models, I wondered, 'Why isn't there a similar simple and effective model for selling?' I searched through my previous sales training manuals, had discussions with colleagues and explored the internet but couldn't find a model that I believed would truly deliver what salespeople (and sales leaders) needed, regardless of market or role.

So I developed my own. It's simple enough to recall instinctively yet comprehensive enough to be of use to all sales professionals, regardless of their experience.

The INSPIRe Secret Sales System is the result of over twenty years of experience in sales, sales leadership, business management, coaching and training. It is trusted by many sales teams and sales managers, and it will help you strengthen the important relationships in your life.

You may be wondering why the Secret Sales System is 'secret'. There are two reasons. The first is that the system is unique. In all the years I served as a sales and business leader, I never found a system that delivered what the INSPIRe Secret Sales System does: the psychology, the skills and the process. The second reason is that, since its inception, the Secret Sales System has been known only to a select few high-performing sales teams who work with me and my team. When selecting clients for training and coaching on the system, we ring-fence customers in key segments, so that they get access to a true competitive advantage. The system has become a valued secret among those key clients.

With the publication of this book, I am sharing the secret to help countless teams and leaders dramatically improve their sales performance. This is a fundamental part of my mission: to transform leadership, inspire teams and create legacies in organisations and communities around the world. I'm delighted to let you in on the secret.

When we inspire someone, we infuse into their mind. We connect and communicate with them deeply, enabling us to influence and engage them in a way that is incredibly valuable. As you review the INSPIRe Secret Sales System, I encourage you to keep this representation of the system ever present in your mind.

The acronym INSPIRe is a mnemonic. Here it is in full:

INSPIRe – Secret Sales System
(Rapport and Relationship)

I – Insight and Impact

N – Needs Discovery

S – Solution Discussion

P – Proposal Agreement

I – Immediate Action

Re – Reflection

The acronym will help you remember, on an un-conscious level, the 'right' process when it comes to selling. It's critical to get the process right – you must perform the right tasks in the right order. I like to use the analogy of flat-pack furniture. You can wing it, but if you don't follow the step-by-step instructions, you inevitably end up with something in the wrong place or the wrong way around or with pieces left over. Sales is exactly like that. If you don't follow a process, you're likely to miss something important that your client needs to make a decision.

Get comfortable with a process

Many salespeople who don't follow a process justify this decision by saying they'll come across as sound-ing scripted. This is just a poor excuse, or a cover-up. It's true that when you first start following the process you may have to concentrate on it – but that's why we use a mnemonic. The acronym makes it easy to remember the order and flow. Once you've practised it (and I recommend that you do, through the exer-cises in each chapter) and it becomes engrained, you won't have to consciously think about it. You will flow through the process. And once you have it committed to your unconscious memory, you will naturally better understand and meet your clients' needs. And you *will* win more business.

For those of you who prefer a visual representation, the flow chart below shows how the process works.

INSPIRe – Secret Sales System

As you can see from the diagram, the process is designed to be ongoing and continuous. It will help you establish a methodology that you can use in all your interactions with people, whether it's a dynamic sales call or as part of building a long-term relationship with a client. You may also have noticed that in the system's second, third and fourth stages, the process flows in both directions. INSPIRe is a fluid system, and each stage must be completed before the next can be successfully progressed through. If you get stuck or your client is resisting, orient yourself to this system and return to the stage that's necessary to get you and your client back on track. You will find answers simply by letting the system guide you.

Once the process is imprinted in your mind, whether you use the acronym or the flow chart or a combination of the two, you will be able to relax and be yourself in your sales interactions with your clients.

Sales Mastery: Roles in your client's organisation

If you're selling to organisations, no matter how large or small, it's important to identify the roles of people working within these organisations. When I use the term 'role', I'm referring to the part they play in the sales and/or decision-making process. Not everyone has the same power, influence or ability when it comes to making decisions. You need to understand 'who's who' so that you can invest the right amount of time with the right people – something all successful salespeople learn to do, either consciously or unconsciously. Of course you'll use your rapport skills to engage and manage your relationships with all the people working within the organisation, but there are additional things to consider when dealing with certain roles.

Gatekeepers

Gatekeepers are people in the organisation who work to ensure time isn't wasted. Specifically, they're in place to prevent people, especially salespeople, from getting to their boss – your client.

How to manage gatekeepers

It's important to build relationships with gatekeepers. You want them to like you and to want to get you in front of the client. Here are a few tips on how to engage them:

- Learn a little about them and personalise the conversation accordingly, eg, 'How's your tennis coming along?'

- Find out something about them you like and genuinely flatter them, eg, 'I thought it was really considerate of you to do that for your colleague.'

- Consider how your product or service would benefit them and tailor your impact statement to them (we'll look at impact statements shortly).

- Use your rapport skills (we'll cover this in the next chapter).

Influencers

Influencers are people in the organisation who will use your product or service and have an opinion about it – an opinion that matters. They will usually be well established in the organisation (a member of the senior team or progressing in that direction). They will be able to influence decisions regarding your product or service.

How to manage influencers

Influencers can help you throughout your sales process, so treat them as you would treat the decision maker (aka your client). They need to be understood and have their needs met. You may want to invite them to be part of the client meeting (if they haven't already been invited). This can be flattering to the influencer and help you get them on board more quickly. If they aren't involved directly in your client meeting, it's worth investing the time to keep them informed of progress and ensure they feel good about your proposals so that they'll support your sales process in the background.

Decision makers

Decision makers will ultimately decide which product or service their organisation signs up for. They can secure your business. They are usually the most senior person in the organisation, or a partner, and have the final say in what goes and what doesn't. This is the key role. Every time you sell, you must understand the decision maker's needs and convince them that your product or service is the best option to meet those needs.

How to manage decision makers

This is your client, so you'll use the INSPIRe Secret Sales System when dealing with the decision maker. We'll cover this later in the book.

Champions

Champions are influencers who absolutely love your product or service – and you! They may also be a decision maker. Champions will rave about your product or service to anyone who will listen. They are likely to have overcome a significant issue with your product or service and/or to have a positive relationship with you or your organisation. They are one of your biggest assets in sales. The more champions you can create (and harness), the faster your business will grow.

How to manage champions

Your champion is likely to be someone you are already managing well, but here are a few useful tips you may not have considered:

- Ask them about their personal interests to deepen your relationship.
- Ask them about their career aspirations and goals.
- Ask about who they know in other organisations or within their network, and if they could introduce you.
- Ask for their permission to use their name as a reference (this can be flattering if done in the right way).
- Ask if there is anyone they would like to get to know (and then see if you or a colleague can make it happen).
- Consider the opportunity for them to champion your product outside of their organisation.
- Discuss opportunities for them to speak on your behalf (as an expert on a relevant topic for your business), or to become a leader in their field.
- Introduce them to your line manager – show them how important they are to you.
- Talk to your manager (or marketing department) about how your organisation might be able to work more collaboratively with them.
- Create some time to get to know them outside of their working environment, perhaps over coffee or lunch (this is surprisingly effective – you'll see a different side to your client).

If you're able to harness your champions, they'll be able to help you broaden your reach and speed up your sales process with new clients, as you'll already have credibility from a referral.

Budget holders

Budget holders are in charge of the finances. They'll know whether your client can afford your product (if they're not also the decision maker), and they'll know if your client has contracts in place or stock to use or other options your client may not have considered. Ultimately, they'll do what the decision maker decides, but they can slow down the process and even create barriers if they aren't supportive of your product or service.

How to manage budget holders

If your budget holder is a decision maker, manage them using the INSPIRe Secret Sales System. If not, you'll need to consider these things:

- Are they a user of the product?
    - If they are, manage them as you would the influencer.
    - If they aren't, ask how involved they are with the product or service (you don't want to sell to them if they're not interested).

- Give them the headlines of why your client has chosen the product or service:

    - '[The client] has [xx] need.'

    - 'Our [product or service] will meet the need better than any other available.'

    - '[The client] has decided that [product or service] will be introduced from [date] into [departments], and we have agreed on a cost of [xx].'

- Check that they are supportive and will process the order in the way agreed with your client.

- Thank them for helping to make the improvement your product or service will deliver.

Remember to confirm with your client that you have met with the budget holder and that everything is progressing as agreed.

Disruptors

As the term suggests, disruptors are those people in your client's organisation who will try to get in the way of your success. They don't want you to win the business. There may be any number of reasons for this: loyalty to a competitor, fear of change, a previous issue with your organisation, maybe they dislike you! Whatever the reason, you need to be aware of them and their intent and be clear on how you'll manage them.

How to manage disruptors

It's important to be respectful of every member of your client's organisation. The disruptor is no exception. Here are some pointers for managing them:

- Be calm, considerate and interested in their position.

- Don't give them any reason to justify their cause/issue/position.

- Understand their rationale, perspective or argument.

- Refer to the objection-handling techniques in Chapter 11.

- Don't agree with them – empathise and seek to understand.

- Consider how they fit in the organisation's hierarchy – find out who they look up to.

- If possible, engage and manage the person who is senior to them (this will influence the disruptor).

In the worst-case scenario, if they just won't change their mind:

- Consider how you can get them to a neutral position.

- Agree to disagree, but appreciate their points.

- Minimise their influence or impact (through more senior relationships).

- Be clear on their objection and how it could be overcome / handled, even if they can't be persuaded.

Some people simply will not see another point of view. Don't be overly concerned. Manage them as best you can and move on.

Time sinks

I've purposely left this role until last. Time sinks may have some influence in your client's organisation, but they'll be a real drain on your time. They will generally be people who have been with the organisation for a long time and are stuck in the same position – they may be bored, less productive and unambitious. They won't necessarily know they're wasting your time and are often quite pleasant people, but ultimately, they won't help you to be successful, now or in the future.

How to manage time sinks

It bears repeating: be respectful of everyone in your client's organisation. Not only is it the right thing to do, but it will also make you feel better about yourself and it will be noticed by your client and their team. Plus, you never know how much influence someone has and where or when you might meet them again, so always be kind! There are a number of techniques you can deploy for managing time wasters:

- Engage with them only as part of a scheduled slot of time and say something along these lines: 'Hi, it's good to see you. I'm on my way to meet with Bill, but I have a couple of minutes. What's up?'

- In advance, think of a legitimate reason to leave your discussion.

- Show just the right amount of interest (but don't be too keen or you'll get yourself stuck).

- Ask questions that get to the point and keep them on track.

- If they get distracted, steer them back on topic.

- Consider asking closed questions to keep the conversation short.

- Know when to leave, be firm and make your exit.

You must be able to identify and manage time sinks appropriately, otherwise they'll slow you down, leave you feeling drained or frustrated, and prevent you from growing your business at the optimal rate.

Before we move on, reflect on this chapter and write down your thoughts in your journal or notebook.

6

Overcoming Challenges

I was working as a sales and marketing manager in a healthcare company. At this point, I had many years of experience under my belt and was well regarded by the organisation and our clients. The organisation had several business development managers (BDMs), who managed large healthcare business accounts. One of the BDMs (we'll call her Grace) secured an important meeting with a procurement director acting on behalf of a customer group. Grace was taking the lead on a procurement project, and the objective of the customer group she was targeting was to identify the lowest-priced, 'fit for purpose' product in a specific category. We were the higher-quality market leader, the group's predominant supplier *and* among the most expensive. The procurement director (let's call her Roberta) was renowned for being demanding and challenging, and neither of us had met her before.

We prepared for the meeting thoroughly and developed numerous questions and a draft proposal that we believed would be compelling. We arrived at the meeting ahead of time and were well briefed, prepared for anything the client could throw at us.

The meeting did not go well!

Roberta did everything in her power to impede our attempts at creating rapport. She scowled all the way through the meeting and snarled when we introduced humour, kept her arms folded, shook her head at every occasion and kept her answers to all of Grace's high-quality questions (more on those later) short and sharp. It was one of the toughest client meetings I've ever experienced – uncomfortable, negative and disheartening.

Roberta's position in a nutshell was that in order for the group to make savings, they couldn't stay with the incumbent – they had to move to a low-priced supplier. I believe we made a compelling case and did everything possible in that meeting. We discussed the costs of change, we provided evidence of the support our sales and clinical teams provided to the group's accounts and we had referrals from senior clinicians across the group who were determined to keep using our products because they firmly believed we were the best supplier. Roberta was unmoved. I'm convinced she'd made up her mind before the meeting – no matter what, we were out!

Our final discussion was about patient safety and included a review of the valuable work our teams had been doing alongside clinicians in their group to improve standards and consistency of care and reduce risk for patients. When I mentioned that these initiatives couldn't be supported by a low-priced competitor (which this competitor subsequently confirmed to Roberta), she said, 'That's a risk I'm prepared to take.' That was the point at which we agreed to wrap up the meeting and leave.

I later learned that this meeting was typical of Roberta's style. Over the next few years, the procurement project didn't gain much traction. The wider group didn't appear to support the decisions made and apparently saw Roberta as someone who made cynical, biased recommendations. My organisation's business didn't change much across the group, but the proposal we made to them would have delivered significant savings for their organisation.

I also learned that in one meeting, Roberta rejected a significant savings proposal in favour of a cheap supplier and terminated an existing agreement (and was rude to a senior manager). Within a couple of months, the product from the cheap supplier was failing. The supplier then ran out of stock. Roberta had no choice but to instruct her team to start sourcing from the original supplier at a much higher price. This is an awful example of how a limited number of procurement people operate. When they don't create working partnerships with their suppliers, they can actually increase their organisational costs.

Learning from difficult clients

We all have difficult clients, and we cannot always win, but I'm grateful for my experience with Roberta. It made me much more aware of how difficult some clients can be, and that I shouldn't take it personally. It was also a reminder that sometimes, you just need to accept a situation and move on to the next, more appreciative, client.

So before we start working with the INSPIRe Secret Sales System, take this opportunity to think about difficult sales or client situations you've found yourself in. Identify what happened and prepare yourself to better handle these types of encounters in the future. Learning to trust the sales system and the skills you develop will really help.

Think of a specific client interaction that didn't go the way you wanted it to. Now keep these questions in mind and reflect on them as you continue to work through the book. You may want to write them down in your journal or notebook so they're handy.

- What was the challenge with the client?

- Which part of the system might I have been missing?

- What should I focus more of my time on when it comes to my clients?

- What am I learning about how I currently sell in comparison to the model?

- What changes could I make?

- What impact would this have on my future performance?

- What am I committed to changing?

Sales Mastery: Your inner voice

Client perspective

Before we meet with, or contact, our clients, there's usually a lot going on in our minds. Our 'inner voice' gets loud and can default to a negative perspective. We might ask ourselves these types of questions:

- What if I can't get them interested?

- How do I win this business?

- What if they ask for something I can't give them?

- What mood will they be in?

- What do I say if they challenge the price?

These thoughts can create stress and pressure and, in turn, impair your performance in the meeting. A simple way to overcome this is to put yourself in your client's shoes. To gain a new perspective and feel more at ease going into your meetings, follow these simple steps:

- Imagine you are your client, in the time before meeting with you.

- Ask yourself:
    - What do I want to get from this meeting?
    - How do I want to be treated by the salesperson?
    - What am I most afraid of?
    - What would win me over?
    - What is *my* ideal outcome?

- Capture your answers in your journal or notebook and consider how these insights might improve your meeting.

This worksheet will be a useful template as we work through the INSPIRe Secret Sales System: https://bit.ly/INSPIRe-Worksheet.

Managing your inner voice

Each of us has an inner voice, and it chatters away most of the time. It's your cheerleader when you're doing well, and it can be your most fearsome critic when you're not. It's not something people tend to talk about or confront often, but because it can be distracting, we must spend time improving it and learning to use it more effectively. In NLP research and theory, a number of principles explain how the mind works. One of them is that *every behaviour has a positive intention*. This is particularly true when it comes to your inner voice. However critical you may find the voice, the intention behind it is always positive. For example, when you put yourself in a difficult situation, your mind will always try to protect you. It will either help you prepare or try to get you to avoid the situation altogether. Unfortunately, the inner voice isn't always useful or empowering, even though that's the intent.

With awareness, time and practice, you can turn your inner critic into your inner coach – a voice that supports you and helps you improve. It can become one of your most powerful and positive allies in your career and your life.

When I'm feeling frustrated with myself, my inner voice will generate rapid-fire negative comments or questions, such as:

- This happens all the time. You're useless.

- How did you get into this mess?

- How much worse can this get?

As soon as I notice the pattern of questions, I catch myself. I stop the thoughts, take a deep breath, check my posture and ask an empowering question, such as:

- Thank you. There's something here for me to learn. What is it?

- What is the positive intention in this for me?

- How can I use this to make me even better in the future?

By making the effort to increase your awareness, you can leverage your inner voice. It's well worth it. Below are four simple steps to help you handle your inner voice:

1. Notice what your inner voice is saying.

2. Acknowledge and thank your inner voice (this takes the power away and gives you control).

3. Ask yourself, 'What is the positive intention in this for me?'

4. Then ask, 'What is the best outcome I can get from this now?'

If this is particularly relevant to you, I urge you to research further.[6]

Before we move on, reflect on this chapter and write down your thoughts in your journal or notebook.

---

6   If you would like to learn more about NLP there are many resources available online. Simply search for 'NLP' and you will be surprised at just how much information, training and content is available.

7
Building Rapport

When I first learned about rapport and relationships as a fundamental part of selling and influencing, it was an important discovery for me. I realised that people like people who are like them. They also like people who are interested in them. At the start of a relationship it's critical to show interest. I remember using this principle with an important new key account customer I was responsible for managing. The first time I had met with him we hadn't 'connected' at all. He had issues with the service my predecessor had been providing and his trust in the company – and by virtue, me – was compromised. At the end of the first meeting the atmosphere was frosty.

At the next meeting I focused solely on building rapport and gaining his trust. As soon as I arrived at his office and we were introduced again I made a conscious effort to act and behave in a similar way to him. I asked questions about him, his work and his team. I asked questions that uncovered the challenges in the previous relationship and questions that led him to tell me how I could 'reset' our relationship. I kept the questions focused on a positive affiliation for both parties, while actively being interested and 'like him'. All the time, I matched his pace, tone, body language and gestures. During the course of the meeting our connection strengthened.

The result was astounding. Over the course of six months and around six meetings, the relationship became one of the strongest I had among all of my clients. I was invited to the company's business events, to join industry groups they ran, to work with their sales and marketing teams (something only key partners were invited to do). I used the entire sales process to turn this relationship around, but a vital foundation was rapport. We must always act to strengthen rapport and our relationships.

This is the last area we'll cover before getting into the specific stages of the sales process: building rapport. Rapport is fundamental when working with clients, which is why it's at the centre of the model. It's necessary throughout every stage. Once you've engaged your client (and even before that, depending on the situation), you must develop rapport and trust. This will ensure the working relationship between you and your client is built on a solid foundation.

INSPIRe – Secret Sales System: Client and Salesperson Relationship

How do we build rapport?

There are many perspectives on rapport, but I see it as the ability to relate to others in a way that creates a level of trust and understanding. Rapport helps build a relaxed, positive relationship. In sales interactions, it enables the client and the salesperson to unconsciously gain agreement and acceptance.

So how do we go about creating it? Here are a few ways to build rapport with clients (as well as with friends, family and colleagues):

• Smile (we'll talk about the flooding smile in the next section)

- Use body language to show openness, trust and understanding

- Be interested – ask genuine questions about the person and their situation

- Make eye contact, especially when the other person is talking

- Listen actively by leaning in and acknowledging what they're saying

- Be grateful and respectful

- Enjoy spending time with them (make a conscious effort to do so)

- Create common ground

- Build trust over time by showing genuine empathy, being present and engaged in all interactions, and doing what you say you'll do

Sales Mastery: Deepening rapport and using emotions

Using your face, body language and voice

In her book *How to Talk to Anyone*, Leil Lowndes explains several ways (ninety-two, in fact) to create rapport and strengthen relationships.[7] The two that

---

7 L Lowndes, *How to Talk to Anyone: 92 little tricks for big success in relationships* (HarperElement, 2014)

are most relevant to deepening our learning about rapport in this chapter are the flooding smile and sticky eyes.

The flooding smile

The technique for the flooding smile is to wait before smiling at the recipient instead of smiling straight away. Look at the person's face for a moment, soak in their persona and then give them a warm, broad smile in response. The evidence suggests that the recipient of this smile will feel as though it's special and just for them, so unconsciously, it will mean more to them. A great start to building rapport!

Sticky eyes

This is a technique for developing better eye contact, which is critical for rapport – eye contact allows you to show genuine interest. Imagine that your eyes are glued to your client with warm, sticky toffee. In conversation, don't break eye contact, even after they've finished speaking (which is our normal conversational behaviour). When you do look away, do it slowly, as if pulling on toffee. If you know someone who makes strong eye contact, you'll know how intense it can be. Early in relationships it enables strong rapport.

There are many other ways to deepen rapport, and we do several of them unconsciously. By becoming more aware of these techniques and actions and using them consciously, you'll put your clients at ease, strengthen your relationships and feel more in control of yourself.

Matching and mirroring

Isn't it interesting how you can watch people talking in a café or restaurant and be able to tell whether or not they're getting along? Body language gives it away. If they have rapport, they'll be unconsciously copying each other's positions, actions and movements. You can do this consciously with your clients. By gradually matching and mirroring your client's body position, arm and hand gestures, posture and distance (leaning in or away), you'll deepen your rapport. With practice, you can increase the speed with which you build rapport with almost anyone. You can even try it at a distance with people you want to engage or influence. Try it and see! Once you've built deep rapport, you can then lead the rapport with your client – you'll move and they'll follow.

Voice

How you say something is just as important as what you say. The way in which we speak – pace, tone and language patterns – allows us to engage other people and strengthen rapport. Your job at the outset is to reflect your client's pace and tone so that you're 'harmonising' with them. Then listen to the language they're using. You don't have to copy it exactly but notice it and use similar patterns. When we spend time with people we like, we start to pick up their words and expressions. You can make a conscious effort to do this with clients. Your rapport will become stronger and your client may even start to use some of your language – the ultimate compliment in rapport!

Remember: rapport is unconscious and reciprocal. If you enjoy an interaction, your client will be drawn to enjoy it too (without even realising it).

Handling the breakdown of rapport

When we're under pressure, we may stop acting naturally and start trying to force ourselves to act differently. As rapport (or loss of it) is unconscious, the other person will instinctively notice a disconnect. You might be able to recall situations where you felt this disconnect yourself, whether it was with a client or when you were a customer or in the company of someone who made you uncomfortable. Once you notice this disconnect, you can re-establish rapport by following these simple steps:

1. Put yourself and the other person at ease by making a light joke or pointing out a distraction you can both focus on.

2. Regain genuine interest in the person. You might apologise for taking the conversation off track and

then ask an open question. For example: 'Sorry, I had to point that out. It was just so interesting. Anyway, you were telling me about your experience with your team. How did that work out for you?'

3. Listen intently and generate empathy for the other person.

4. Lean in and show your interest.

5. Ask simple, expansive questions (you might be surprised by how effectively these keep a conversation flowing):

   - Wow, tell me more about that.

   - What else happened?

   - What happened next?

   - How did that make you feel?

6. Once the conversation flows again, match your client's body language.

It really can be this simple. With practice, it will become easier and easier to build and strengthen your rapport, even with the most difficult people.

A different perspective on rapport

Think about how easy it is to spend time with close friends and family. In a relaxed environment, with no pressure, you're likely using some, if not all, of the techniques in this section about rapport without realising it. Now that you're aware, you can consciously improve your rapport-building skills.

In Chapters 3 and 4 we looked at visualising a positive outcome. Visualisation will also prime you to naturally generate the kind of rapport you need with your clients. When it comes to building rapport with clients you may find difficult, try this visualisation technique.

EXERCISE: AMONG FRIENDS

1. Imagine you're catching up with a close friend over a drink.
2. Notice the way you interact with each other – how easy it is and how relaxed you both are.
3. Think about what you see, what you hear and what you feel.
4. Now imagine the client sitting with you and your friend.
5. Imagine them joining the discussion, enjoying the time with you and your friend.
6. Notice how this changes your perception of them.

After completing this exercise, you'll likely notice a difference in the way you think/feel about and act towards this client. Answer these questions in your journal or notebook:

- What have I learned?
- What will I commit to changing?
- What will my client and I gain as a result?

If you want to learn more, there are plenty of books on rapport, body language and relationship building.[8] This subject is fascinating, and it's worth investing your time in it.

Rapport – a counter note

There may be times when you don't want to build rapport – maybe someone has annoyed you or you want to end a conversation or you're the subject of un-wanted attention. You can consciously break rapport by doing the opposite of everything recommended in this chapter so far. Remember, rapport is unconscious. If you consciously break it, the other person will feel uncomfortable and, unless they're a self-obsessed megalomaniac, find it hard to stick around. The quick-est way to break rapport is to:

- Avoid eye contact

- Fold your arms (use 'closed' body language)

- Don't ask any questions

- Don't show any interest in them

- Turn your body away from them and look to engage someone else

---

8   Two I recommend as a great place to start are: D Carnegie, *How to Win Friends and Influence People* (Vermilion, 2006), and J Borg, *Body Lan-guage: How to know what's really being said*, third edition (Pearson, 2013)

Using emotions

This might sound like an odd topic to include in a sales manual, but most purchase decisions are based on emotion, not logic – though many clients will believe they're buying based on logic and will have objective reasons to support their buying decisions. When you're selling to your client, keep in mind that everyone buys to satisfy their feelings – feelings associated with the product/service, the company and the salesperson. To be more consistently successful when you're selling, tap into emotions and evoke powerful feelings in your client. To do so, it's important to establish three fundamentals in your client relationship:

- Trust – you do what you say you'll do (to satisfy your client)

- Confidence – you have the experience and abilities (you're their best choice)

- Support – you have concern for their needs (during and after the sale)

As you learn about the INSPIRe Secret Sales System, you'll see how you can leverage the power of emotions to better serve your clients and ensure your success in meeting their needs. Your ability to question your clients and position your solution according to their needs will set you and your organisation apart from competitors. Whatever you're selling, consider these questions, which will help you develop your emotional-selling capability. Capture your answers in your journal or notebook.

- What is the greatest positive impact working with me will have on my client?

- What is the greatest obstacle I can enable my clients to overcome?

- How grateful will my client be for my support?

- How far and wide is the impact of working with me for my client and their organisation/life?

- What are the words and feelings my client would use to express their gratitude?

Reflect on your answers to these questions, as they'll help you tap into the motivation you need to stay connected to your client's emotions. This in turn will help you to meet their needs more effectively. Remember, people buy on emotions, in an effort to satisfy their feelings. By helping them do this, you're meeting their needs beyond the sales process.

Before we move on, reflect on this chapter and write down your thoughts in your journal or notebook.

OPTIONAL EXERCISE: BUILDING RAPPORT

Look for opportunities to practise intentional deepening of rapport. It may be with someone you don't get on with well; it may be at social gatherings or with work colleagues. Start to notice what happens when you develop rapport and how you can 'lead' the other person in actions and conversation.

When you've gained confidence, try and tackle more difficult people with this approach of 'rapport first'. Think of someone with whom it has been challenging for you to connect, and try using your rapport-deepening skills and practices. You'll be surprised at how you can win these people over and gain a deeper connection with them when you take this approach.

PART THREE

THE SALES SYSTEM

8

Insight And Impact

INSPIRe - Secret Sales System: Insight and Impact

At the second dental company I worked for, I had a sales colleague who was confident, experienced and funny (we'll call him Roger). He joined the company shortly after I did and was new to the dental industry. After he'd been with the company for about six months, he was accompanied by the managing director (MD) on a 'dual calling' field sales day. If you're in sales, you'll know how nerve-wracking these types of days are, especially when you're relatively new. On their first call together (a dental practice), Roger and the MD were met with a frosty receptionist whose body language made it clear she wasn't impressed that they had turned up unannounced.

Sensing the cold front, Roger made a bold decision. He put on a serious face and said, 'Good morning, we're from Her Majesty's Revenue and Customs, and we're here to see Dr Bannister to inspect his books.' Well, the receptionist went white with shock! She explained that Dr Bannister had a full patient list and that this would wreak havoc on their work that day, and so on, and so on.

Roger then let a large smile creep across his face and said, 'How pleased would you be to see a couple of dental reps right now?' The receptionist fell back in her chair and smiled with relief. She called Roger a 'cheeky devil' and asked him to take a seat, saying, 'I'll fit you in when I can.' Roger and the MD made quite an impression on both the receptionist and the dentist, who also found Roger's introduction hilarious. The story became legendary in the company and the industry, and so did Roger.

Now I'm not suggesting that you do this yourself. It was a huge risk that might not have paid off, but it does illustrate a couple of important points about first impressions: it's important to make a memorable first impression, and you can use humour to disarm people.

Let's look more closely at first impressions before we dive into the sales process.

First impressions

You've probably heard the saying 'you only get one chance to make a first impression'. Well, it's absolutely true. Research suggests that most people make a judgement about someone within seven seconds of meeting them.[9] While it's possible to get a relationship back on track if the first impression isn't good, a not-so-great first impression takes time to correct. Why leave it to chance? It's important to get it right.

In his brilliant book *How to Win Friends and Influence People*, Dale Carnegie outlines several ways to create bonds with people quickly. If you haven't read it, I recommend it. One of Carnegie's suggestions is to consciously use a person's name over and over, in an appropriate way. This helps you and the other person to become familiar with each other and creates a

---

9   'First Impressions', *Psychology Today*, no date, www.psychologytoday. com/intl/basics/first-impressions, accessed 28 September 2020

connection.[10] This is effective in all kinds of situations. When you're in a bar or restaurant, noticing an employee's name and then using it will make a positive impression on them. You might even get better service or preferential treatment. Try it for yourself and see.

Humour

Using humour appropriately can help you build client relationships. You can use the INSPIRe Secret Sales System to amplify your sense of humour, uniqueness and personality. Once you're confident that you have structure in place, your own humour becomes a valuable complement to the process you're using. One-liners, funny stories, well-timed jokes and/or anecdotes are an important part of being yourself with your clients. Once you relax and use the process, you can use humour as you would with family and friends to engage your client. You can increasingly 'be yourself' and let your sense of humour shine through – whatever that means for you. Just make sure you keep things professional and appropriate.

One study looked specifically at the use of humour to get clients to pay more. They found that when salespeople used jokes and humour, the buyer was willing to pay a higher price![11] It seems you can put a price on laughter.

10   D Carnegie, *How to Win Friends and Influence People* (Vermilion, 2006)
11   K O'Quin and J Aronoff, 'Humor as a technique for social influence', *Social Psychology Quarterly*, 44/4 (1981), 349–357

Introducing yourself

Here's some useful guidance on introducing yourself during a sales call:

- Beforehand, plan what you'll say and how you'll say it. Ask yourself, 'How would I want someone to introduce themselves to me if I were the client?'

- Speak clearly, concisely and positively.

- Ensure your introduction is warm and friendly – and smile (even if you're on the phone).

- Say your client's name (and your name and the company name on first meeting).

Now that you've made your first impression, you're ready to create value. It's time to explore insight and impact.

Generate and tailor

Insight is information that's directly relevant to your client. The idea is to research and discover facts, data and/or opinions that aren't common knowledge but could be incredibly valuable to your client. Once you've uncovered your insight, tailor it to your client so that it has impact for them (ie it's meaningful to them).

Insight and impact can take many forms, depending on your marketplace, your product/service and your clients. To generate insight, consider reviewing the following:

- Their marketplace (trends, data, future directions)
- Their clients, patients and/or followers (research, feedback, opinions, demographics)
- Their peers, competitors and/or key opinion leaders (best practices, successes, new evidence, new interpretations)
- A hidden opportunity or threat (data-driven calculations, financial models, whole-life costs, etc)

In my sales training and coaching for companies I often discuss sales process management and sales skills as priority development areas that will drive an increase in sales performance. I start with insight and impact.

A direct link has been found between effective pipeline management and strong revenue growth, yet research by Vantage Point Performance and the Sales Management Association has found that 44% of executives feel they are ineffective at managing their sales pipeline.[12] Companies that mastered the following three skills saw 28% higher revenue growth:

---

12   J Jordan and R Kelly, 'Companies with a formal sales process generate more revenue', *Harvard Business Review*, 2015, https://hbr.org/2015/01/companies-with-a-formal-sales-process-generate-more-revenue#:~:text=On%20average%2C%20companies%20that%20reported,saw%2028%25%20higher%20revenue%20growth, accessed 28 September 2020

1. Clearly defining the sales process

2. Spending a minimum of three hours per month on managing their pipeline

3. Training sales managers on pipeline management

Most people are unaware of these facts. But what do they mean for the client? That's where impact comes in. I would say something like this to the client:

'As you can see, focusing on a few simple things will have a significant impact on business growth. I'd like to discuss how these could benefit you, and how I can help your leaders and teams focus to deliver growth.'

Make notes on your worksheet on what you might include in your impact statement. This will create a template you can use when engaging your client in the early stages of your relationship. Here's the link to the worksheet again: https://bit.ly/INSPIRe-Worksheet.

You can revisit this tool whenever you need to look for insight and create impact statements. They're vital when launching new products or services or when attending trade shows and exhibitions.

Sales Mastery: Make yourself invaluable

As you develop your skills in this area, learn to continually research the field most relevant to your clients. Start to look into the future and not at the past or present. Learn from the thought leaders in your client's field. Learn what they are predicting will happen and share these insights with your clients. Start to see yourself as someone who is continually starting each client interaction with insight and impact. However long you've been seeing your clients, use this approach to make sure the relationship is one of continual value for your client.

When you master this approach and it becomes part of your ongoing discussions with your clients, they will start to see you as a valuable resource and a partner in their business.

So, you're in a client meeting (or you have the client on a phone or video call). You've engaged them with the insight you've gained and your impact statement, and they're keen to learn more about how they can benefit from what you've explained so far. You're in a strong position. What comes next is a step in a different direction for most people. The next step is where the magic happens.

Before we move on, reflect on this chapter and write down your thoughts in your journal or notebook.

OPTIONAL EXERCISE: IMPACT STATEMENT

This practical exercise is one I use with clients and is designed to be practised with a colleague (preferably someone who also wants to practise their sales technique).

Use your client scenario from Chapter 6 (the challenging client you've identified). Decide who will be the client and who will be the salesperson. The salesperson will then brief the client on the scenario, explain the challenge the client presents and what your objectives are for the meeting.

Practise delivering your introduction and impact statement.

Discuss with your colleague how it sounds. Keep practising until delivering it sounds and feels natural to you. Ask your colleague to say it to you too. How impactful is it?

Keep working on it until you create an impact statement that gives you what you need to engage your clients and kickstart your sales process.

9

Needs Discovery

INSPIRe – Secret Sales System: Needs Discovery

From late 2004 until 2010, I worked as a sales manager with a medical sales team in the South of England selling medical devices to healthcare organisations

(I really enjoyed the healthcare marketplace and customers). My sales team and I worked in the field regularly.

One day we had a client meeting in London. The client was a senior nurse (we'll call him Pete), and we were meeting to discuss how we might better support him in his work while exploring opportunities for our portfolio. Pete was a highly experienced nurse who'd been 'worn down' (his words) by the work. He felt exasperated, powerless and exhausted. The salesperson I was working with asked Pete questions about his priorities and long-term aspirations, and Pete's answers were incredibly negative. To be honest, it was quite depressing! I had recently qualified as an NLP practitioner and was interested in his body language, emotional state and language. Having a sense that there was a way to turn the meeting around, I recalled something I'd learned in the NLP programme. It was a question I repeated to myself when I was feeling stumped, lost or in need of inspiration, and I still use it to this day. 'What is the best question I can ask right now?' It's an invaluable prompt for creating a change in my own mental state and others'.

I looked at Pete and my salesperson and asked, 'Do you mind if I ask a question?' The salesperson looked relieved (this is a useful way to change a subject or create a change in a conversation – simply ask permission to do so, and you'll rarely get declined).

'Pete, what's been your greatest achievement in the last twelve months? The thing you're most proud of?'

He looked surprised then quickly said, 'There isn't anything. It's been a terrible year.'

'So, you're telling me that in the whole of the last year, there isn't anything you've achieved at work that you're proud of?'

This seemed to shock him again. There was a silence while he thought long and hard. I signalled to the salesperson to stay quiet. Finally, Pete said, 'Well, there's the patient audit we did this year.'

I feigned a look of surprise. 'A patient audit? Please tell me more about that.'

He went on to tell us about the project he'd led – a trust-wide audit of over 1,000 patients occupying beds in the organisation. He explained how he'd coordinated a significant piece of work and then used the data that came from it to build a business case – which led to an investment, which was used to upgrade the beds across the trust. The follow-up audit revealed that this had significantly positively impacted the quality of care for patients. A truly impressive achievement, but one he'd forgotten about.

The meeting transformed. Once Pete had tapped into the positive event and was explaining it and experiencing it again, everything changed – his posture, his body language, his attitude. Everything. The salesperson and I were genuinely impressed and complimented him on leading such a significant programme. We ended up uncovering a significant opportunity that complemented his recent work and would deliver benefits to his service and future patient treatment. In that same meeting, we secured a follow-up meeting with him and the procurement team to make sure that our product evaluation would get the right support from the outset (an important lesson he'd learned from the audit programme). That account became one of the largest ones for our business.

It *is* possible to turn around difficult client meetings (and clients). When you ask the right questions, you can help your clients in ways they don't realise are possible. You can create opportunities that have benefits that are far reaching for your clients, for you and for the industry in which you operate. Your potential in a professional sales role goes far beyond success in sales. If you want to, you can make a real difference in the world.

Resist the urge to pitch

So, back to our sales system. You're over the first hurdle – you're through the door and in the meeting. You've delivered a powerful impact statement, you've established rapport and your client is engaged.

Congratulations, you're off to a great start. This is where it's really tempting to jump into pitching.

Don't do it!

In my experience, when relationships between sales-people and clients don't work, this is the point at which it breaks down. After a strong start, you need to build on that momentum with needs discovery through questioning and listening. This is arguably the most important stage of the system for a number of reasons. It will:

- Build the foundation for your sale

- Unlock your client's priorities, challenges and needs

- Give you a window into your client's world

- Strengthen your rapport with the client

- Show you how your client thinks

- Help you understand what your client likes and, importantly, what they don't like

- Help you identify the best way to position your solution (and how not to)

- Enable you to better understand how you can truly satisfy your client

The challenge at this stage is that it can feel as if you're delaying because it falls to the client to do most of the talking. But don't be fooled. You're not delaying – you're learning. Enjoy this part of the process. It is, without a doubt, the most valuable time you can invest in your client meeting. You may have heard the expression 'You have two ears and one mouth so that you can listen twice as much as you speak'. This is particularly relevant during this part of the sales process. This is the time to learn our clients' motivations, needs and reasons to buy.

In Chapter 1, we looked at the three important components of your client proposition. Here's a recap. Remember, they'll be assessing and questioning:

1. You, the salesperson

2. Your product or service

3. Your organisation

This is the ideal time to learn exactly what your client is looking for from you, from your product/service and from your organisation. Find out as much as you can about them and their needs. You can do this only by *questioning, listening* and *responding*.

We'll walk through each of these one at a time, but before we do, let's look at another valuable technique.

Pre-framing and contracting for confidentiality

Before we start questioning and listening, the core of our Needs Discovery stage, we should consider pre-framing. This is an advanced sales skill that few salespeople use and something I only discovered after working as a business coach. The principle of pre-framing is to create a safe yet challenging environment for you and your client. It calls for you to be bold and confident and to take an assertive position in the relationship with your clients. Here's how it works.

There are three key components to pre-framing:

1. Your client's needs

2. Confidentiality

3. Permission

We'll look at them in order.

Your client's needs

At this stage you may not know all of your client needs, but through your preparation, insight and impact statement, you know what grabs their attention. The first stage of pre-framing is to reference what you know about your client.

Confidentiality

This is important: committing to confidentiality with your client quickly and effectively creates a bond of trust. You are making a commitment to keep the client's comments and information completely confidential between the two of you. This rapidly creates a contract or agreement between you that connects and strengthens the relationship.

Permission

Finally, with trust formed, you can ask your client permission to enquire about them, their business, their team, their clients, their goals, their dreams, their desires, their fears – almost anything you feel it's important to understand so you can help them in the most valuable way possible.

It's important to note: once you commit to confidentiality with a client, you must take the responsibility that comes with this agreement seriously. This is an investment in the relationship and will create a bond like no other principle can.

How it works

Here's an example from my own client pre-framing of how the technique can work:

ME: You've said how important it is to you to grow your business, without compromising the quality of service to your clients and while keeping your team fully engaged. Is that right?

CLIENT: Yes, that's right.

ME: I'd like to have a conversation with you in complete confidence. I won't share anything we discuss with anybody else; the details will remain confidential between the two of us. Would that be OK?

CLIENT: Yes, that's fine by me.

ME: OK, with that agreed, would it be OK if I asked you a few questions about the business, so I can help you meet your goals?

CLIENT: Yes, sure. What would you like to know?

In my experience, this is how the conversation always goes. I have never had a client say no to this approach. I start every client conversation with this approach and it creates a depth that no other method can. Try it – you might be surprised how effective it is.

What about existing clients?

I've been asked this question before, so I wanted to address it. The answer is that to pre-frame with existing clients, you need to 'reset' the relationship. Here's how.

Next time you have a meeting with your client, after you have established rapport, make a statement along these lines: 'There's something I really wish I'd asked you a long time ago, that I think would be valuable for you…'. You can now carry out the pre-frame as previously described.

Your client is primed. Now let's get started with questioning.

Questioning (high-quality questions)

It's a fact: not all questions are created equal. There's a clear distinction between high-quality questions (HQQs) and all other questions. While it may not be possible to ask HQQs all the time, you should strive to do so as often as possible in your client interactions. You'll see a number of examples in this chapter and will also get the chance to create a few of your own. Once you've worked through the exercises and identified the HQQs that you think will produce the best results for you, you can improve your client meetings significantly.

HQQs will put you on a fast track to learning about your clients' dreams, emotions and current and future needs, challenges and priorities. You can naturally build on these questions, and they'll unlock information you may not have believed you could get from your clients.

HQQs generally fall into one of three categories:

- Open
- Closed
- Probing

All three are useful throughout the sales system, but they're particularly important in the Needs Discovery stage. The key is to understand when to ask each type of question and to become more aware of the questions you currently ask. Let's look at each more closely.

Open questions

These are the most useful in terms of getting your client talking and opening up to you. They are expansive questions that help you to gain a greater understanding – they encourage people to respond with information, creating conversational flow.

Open questions generally start with one of these words:

- What
- How
- Who
- Where
- When
- Why (only in reverse)

Simply say 'what' or 'how' at the start of any question you ask and you will have created an effective open question. These words will help you elicit more information from your client (or anyone else) than almost all others. Once you form the habit of starting your HQQs with 'what' or 'how', you'll open up a new world of information. Quiet people will become talkers – the secret lies in the questions you ask. If you're finding that certain clients 'dry up' on you, master open questions. You'll give your sales interactions a new lease of life. Plan your open questions in advance to make them even more powerful.

'Who' is also useful when you want to understand decision makers and their influence, and when you're interested in the people who influence your client (their network, peers, mentors, industry experts, etc.).

'Who', 'where' and 'when' can be used to generate *clarifying* open questions, when you need to be clear on your client's decision-making process, the other people involved and the best way to move forward. For example:

- **Who** else should I include on the email?

- **Where** is the best place to send the details?

- **When** are you planning to make the final decision?

While these words will create an open question, they won't open up your client discussions the way that 'what' and 'how' will.

A note about 'why'

'Why' allows you to dig deep – fast! It's personal and powerful. But when using 'why', you must take great care. It might generate negative responses because it can:

- Seem like an accusation and make your client uncomfortable

- Be misinterpreted as a negatively positioned question

- Create distance between you and the client

- Evoke strong negative emotions in your client

- Cause your client to get defensive about themselves or their decisions

- Interfere with the rapport you've built

A good principle to follow if you want to use a 'why' question is to use it in reverse or to discover your client's passion. This means using it when you want your client to defend or compliment you, or if you want them to speak more deeply about their own desires or passions. These questions work best when rapport is strong, the client is onside and you are confident there is good potential for working together.

The why questions could be structured like this.

To encourage the client to compliment you:

- Why would you choose to work with me?

- Why would you consider changing from your current supplier?

- Why do you think working with me would improve your current situation?

To unlock the client's desires and passions:

- Why is it important that you succeed?

- Why do you do the work you do?

- Why do you love your work so much?

- Why are you so committed to your work/team/ business/clients?

You can see that these 'why' questions will elicit a positive emotional response, one that will increase the closeness of your relationship with your client.

Objective questions

You can use 'what' or 'how' in place of 'why' to make your questions more objective. If, for example, you ask your client, 'Why did you decide to do that?' they'll likely feel as if they need to defend their decision. If instead you ask, 'How did you make that decision?' or 'What things did you consider when you were making that decision?' you seem more objective and are likely to gather information much more freely from your clients.

High-quality questions bank

Here are some examples of HQQs that will help you unlock your client's needs, motivations, challenges and priorities. The list isn't exhaustive but will give you some good ideas for your client meetings.

- Where do you see your business in five years?

- How would you describe your vision for your business?

- What is your highest priority this year?

- What is the achievement you're most proud of?

- What was your greatest learning?

- What could get in the way of your plans?

- What are your three biggest challenges?

- What contingencies have you put in place?

- What are the big decisions you'll have to make this year?

- What criteria will you use to make those decisions?

- Who is helping and supporting you?

- Who is involved in the decision-making process?

- What have you found most difficult?

- What are you most afraid of?

- What keeps you awake at night?

- If we had to choose one thing to focus on today / this week / this month, what would it be?

- How do you like to work with supplier organisations?

- Who would you consider to be 'best in class'?

- What do they do that works so well?

- What is it about them you like?

- What would you advise me to do to improve my service to you?

- How would you describe your network in the industry / profession?

- Who is your most trusted professional associate / mentor?

- How do you both benefit from your working relationship?

- If you were me, what would you ask yourself?

- If you could change one thing, what would it be? (More on this one later in the chapter.)

You can find the document containing the high-quality questions bank here: http://bit.ly/HQQ-Bank. It also includes space for you to create your own HQQs. This bank will give you a strong foundation for questioning and should stimulate your thinking about how to develop your questioning skills.

Now let's get practical. Think about your situation, your clients, your business and your product/service. Then create several of your own high-quality (open) questions (using 'what', 'how' and 'who') that would help you better understand your clients' businesses, needs, motivations and decision-making criteria.

In your journal or notebook, write down ten questions starting with 'what' and 'how'. These example questions will be a useful guide before client meetings.

Closed questions

The answer to a closed question is either 'yes' or 'no'. The only time you should use closed questions in your client meetings is when you're:

- Clarifying or checking an answer (Did you mean this?)

- Confirming information (I have this written down – is that right?)

- Making a commitment to move forwards (Are you happy for me to process the order as agreed?)

In these circumstances, it's valuable to use closed questions. Any other time, they will shut down your client conversations, stifle your meetings and even create difficult silences. As a sales manager (and coach), I continue to be surprised by the number of closed questions salespeople use. Unfortunately, they seem to come more naturally than open questions. But if you're someone who asks a lot of closed questions, don't worry – with awareness and practice, you can easily change this behaviour. And the impact is truly transformational.

Reflect on your own questioning skills. If you find yourself in situations where your clients or friends stop talking or answer 'yes' or 'no', you're asking closed questions.

Closed questions will start with these words:

- Have
- Will
- Can
- Do
- Did
- Are
- Is

Remember, closed questions have their place, but you must use them at the right time – not when you're trying to 'open up' a conversation or meeting.

Consider the structure of these questions and the different types of answers they would elicit from you or your clients:

- 'Are you OK?' versus 'How are you?'

- 'Can I make an appointment?' versus 'What would be the best way to make an appointment?'

- 'Do you have any feedback on the proposal?' versus 'What are your thoughts on the proposal?'

- 'Do you like your current product/service?' versus 'How would you improve your current product/service?'

- 'Anything else?' versus 'What else?'

Notice how similar the questions sound but how different the answers to them would be.

Make a note in your journal or notebook about how you'll remind yourself to distinguish between open and closed questions and when you need to use them.

Probing questions

Probing questions can be either open or closed, but they'll allow you to gain further information:

information that many other people might not ask for. Probing allows you to fully understand the specific needs of your client and delve deeper into the important parts of their world – in particular, their priorities, emotions and challenges. Probing is about not taking things at face value. Sometimes you get a sense that there's more to your client than they're telling you. This is when it's appropriate to probe. A lot of salespeople are so keen to get to the sale that they don't take the time to really understand their clients. This is what probing will allow you to do.

Probing questions can be simple and take different forms. The key when probing is to be genuinely interested, lean in and use one or both of these phrases in turn:

• Please, tell me more.

• What else?

These two simple phrases are well known to evoke deeper thoughts and are used widely in coaching. Used in sales, they will help you to gain more insight and a deeper connection with your clients and their needs.

In your journal or notebook, describe how you intend to use these in your sales interactions.

The magic question

Clients can sometimes be resistant to change, and finding a way to get them to see beyond their current practice or ways of working can be difficult. But when you're trying to get clients to consider improvements to their current product, provider, service or solution, you have a powerful tool at your disposal – this question:

> If you could change one thing about your current/past service (or solution or product), what would it be?

This question will stimulate your client's thinking. It's rare to encounter a situation where the client wouldn't change one thing. Once they tell you that 'one thing', get them committed to changing it. You do that by probing. Remember, it's about digging deep and truly understanding the client's issue and how much value there is in solving it.

The structure of this question is also worth reviewing. It's a presupposition – in other words, a presumption of information or facts. Here's an example of how I've used this structure:

> 'Say you had selected my company as the winning supplier. What would I have done to convince you to choose us?'

This question does several things:

- It takes the client forward, beyond the decision they're making.

- It gets them to imagine you as the winning client.

- It helps them to get clear on their priorities and what they want from a supplier.

- It gives you higher-quality information and feedback.

- It strengthens the client's buy-in to you and your organisation.

A real win-win scenario!

A third-party perspective

Sometimes, your client just won't play ball, even if you're asking HQQs. They won't commit to an answer and they won't admit that they have an issue or a need. In these situations, it can be useful to share a third-party perspective. Simply put, tell them that other clients have this specific issue or need. In my experience, this seems to relieve the pressure on the client. Up to that point, they might have felt that they had to admit to a bad decision or to some type of incompetence. As soon as you move the issue or need to another client, your client might find it easier to admit that they're dealing with the same thing. This simple statement can unlock a defensive or resistant client: 'Yes, a number of clients have approached me with this specific issue, and they were surprised by how easily we were able to help them resolve it.'

Once your client admits to having the same issue, ask questions. You need to understand how it affects them personally.

Sales Mastery: Listen, take notes and summarise

Learning to listen

Remember that expression 'You have two ears and one mouth so that you can listen twice as much as you speak'? It's worth repeating here. It's a good way to remember just how important listening is in your client interactions. Listening is a learned skill, and it's not as easy as it sounds. In long client meetings, it can be a challenge to stay focused on listening. But when you ask HQQs, you *must* listen, consciously and intently, to your client's answers. If you don't, there's no point asking questions.

As with any skill or development area, we can improve our listening skills through awareness, a desire to change, and practice. Here are some examples of the blocks to listening that you may or may not be aware of:

- Presuming or mind reading (guessing what will be said next)

- Filtering (leaving out pieces of information)

- Waiting to speak (having your response or next question ready)

- Mind wandering (losing track of the conversation, getting distracted)

- Bringing it back to yourself (taking in everything that was said and then referencing your own experience)

- Interrupting the speaker (not allowing the person to finish)

- Changing the subject (directing the conversation towards a topic you want to discuss)

- Being impatient (showing your irritation)

- Overemphasising (listening too actively, so that it becomes insincere)

You may know people who display these listening blocks, or you may display them yourself. To improve your listening skills, you must be self-aware, so take a moment to reflect on your own blocks when it comes to listening to your clients.

Which do you need to work on most? Write them down in your journal or notebook.

A well-recognised model – described particularly well in the book *Co-Active Coaching*, by Henry Kimsey-House, Karen Kimsey-House and Phillip Sandahl[13] – defines three levels of listening that can help you become a more active listener. Here's my interpretation:

- **Level 1 – Internal listening (conversational):**

  - Listening while waiting to speak

  - Your own inner voice is commentating

  - Giving your own opinion and sharing stories

- **Level 2 – Listening to understand (one-way):**

  - Completely focused on your client

  - Only asking questions that are relevant to them

  - Listening to truly deepen understanding

  - Speaking only to clarify or reflect what you've heard

- **Level 3 – Global Listening (beyond the words):**

  - Listening to more than just the words that are said

  - Noticing body language

---

13 H Kimsey-House, K Kimsey-House and P Sandahl, *Co-Active Coaching: The proven framework for transformative conversations at work and in life*, fourth edition (Aladdin, 2018)

- Listening for tonality and accentuation of words

- Sensing energy levels, feelings and emotions

- Trusting your instincts to guide your responses and questions

When you are meeting with your clients you may start your conversation with level 1 listening. Once you have started the Needs Discovery stage it's critical to consciously listen at levels 2 and 3 – this will require a concerted effort.

Here are my top five tips to improve your listening and more consistently listen at levels 2 and 3:

1. Set yourself a 'level 2 and 3 listening challenge' before each client meeting.

2. Use the sticky eyes technique that we looked at in the Sales Mastery section for 'Deepening rapport and using emotions'.

3. Nod, lean in and mirror your client's body language (be interested and show it).

4. Reflect, repeat and paraphrase the key words your client uses.

5. Notice, acknowledge and silence your own inner voice.

Repeating and paraphrasing

It's important to repeat key words that your client uses. In doing so, you're acknowledging that you're listening and also reinforcing on an unconscious level that you truly understand what the client is telling you. Once you deliberately set out to repeat your client's words and paraphrase what they've said, you'll be compelled to listen more actively. The more you do it, the better you'll get – and this skill will improve many areas of your life. Start practising with everyone you meet from now on.

There is a direct link between listening and body language. It's worth rereading the section in Chapter 7 on body language once you've completed this chapter.

The power of silence

It may seem obvious, but to listen, you must be silent. This is not as easy as it sounds. Many of us have negative associations with silence, perhaps because of childhood experiences in schools, museums or churches or time spent with older relatives. We can also find silence uncomfortable, especially if we spend a lot of time with people who like to talk. For some, there is only silence when they sleep! But if you can become more aware of silence and when to use it, you'll be granted greater insight in your relationships.

Remaining silent after asking a question shows the ultimate respect for the other person. It's a gift you can give them that will be repaid to you a hundred times over with information and a deeper understanding of your client. It's said that during a negotiation, once an offer or request is made, the person who speaks first has already lost. While this isn't always true, being silent after you've asked a question or made an important statement is a vital part of listening. The higher the quality of your questions, the more your client will have to think in order to answer them. Don't rush them. You need to give them time to process the question and come up with the right answer so that you can help to meet their needs – needs they may not realise they have. Give them space with your silence.

By being silent, you:

- Allow your client to reflect, think and process
- Create space for commitment (and give yourself space to think as well)
- Show respect and build further trust
- Improve your chances of success

Here's an interesting fact: 'listen' and 'silent' are made up of the same letters – something to think about before a client interaction!

Notes on note-taking

There are two schools of thought on note-taking in client meetings and interactions.

1. It interferes with your interaction, creates a barrier to rapport and distracts you from important non-verbal cues.

2. It's critical to capturing the client's needs, challenges and priorities. If you're not taking notes, the client might think you're not taking them seriously or truly listening to and understanding them.

I recommend adopting a blend of these opposite views. Here's some guidance to consider when taking notes:

- Before the meeting, write down your objectives and key questions/headings (this will give you a structure for your notes).

- At the start of the meeting, explain to your client that you'll take notes on important points and actions to make sure you better meet their needs.

- Only write down headlines or critical information (not everything said).

- Capture your client's words precisely. Their language is exactly that – theirs –and your interpretation won't be as powerful to them as their own.

- While taking notes, pause to make eye contact and maintain rapport with your client. Check what you've written as you go along, by asking checking questions of your client.

- When you're not writing, put down the pen to show you're listening. Also, you may want to put down your pen if your client makes an important point. This dramatic pause will show you've understood the point (this can be very impactful).

- Be conscious that your notes are creating a structure you can use as a summary at the end of the meeting.

Let's look at this idea of summarising.

Summarising

Once you've asked your questions and listened to the answers, and you believe that you fully understand your client's needs, review your notes and summarise the discussion with your client. Summarising is important because it:

- Gives you greater relevance in the eyes of your client

- Shows you've been listening and that you truly understand what they need

- Creates a natural conversational flow into your discussion on solutions

I suggest you use this format:

- Ask your client for permission to summarise what they've told you (they will always agree).

- Work through your notes. Read them out loud and put a tick next to each of the needs your client told you.

- Clarify each point immediately after you've read it aloud, eg, 'Did I capture that correctly?'

- After you've worked through all your notes, check to make sure nothing has been forgotten. Ask the client, 'Have we covered everything?'

Once your client has agreed that everything has been covered, ask for permission to move on to presenting your solutions. I suggest a joining statement such as this:

'This has been really useful. Thank you for sharing this with me. I'm really pleased with what you've told me. I believe there are a number of ways in which I/ we can help you with the things you've explained. I'd like to share some of those with you now – would that be OK?'

At this stage, we use a closed question because we want permission to move forward. If you've covered everything, your client will be ready to hear what you have to say. It's time for the Solutions Discussion stage.

Take some time to review your worksheet and make note of the HQQs you want to ask in your client meetings. This will help you build your own INSPIRe Secret Sales System.

Before we move on, reflect on this chapter and write down your thoughts in your journal or notebook.

OPTIONAL EXERCISE: QUESTIONS

Continue the optional exercise from the previous chapter.

Practise:

- Delivering your introduction and impact statement
- Asking open and probing questions
- Asking the magic question ('If you could change one thing...')
- Summarising your client's needs in their language
- Confirming you've covered everything

10
Solutions Discussion

INSPIRe – Secret Sales System: Solutions Discussion

When I was working for a large corporate as a business manager, we sold a visual privacy filter. This IT security product is a plastic sheet designed to fit the screen of a laptop or PC. When you look at the screen directly you can see right through the sheet. As soon as you move to the left or right the view is obscured – this creates 'visual security'. There are many types on the market. We had a range that we offered to our distribution partners, for them to sell to their business and enterprise clients.

One of our distributors received a sizeable order that their client wanted fulfilled extraordinarily quickly. Together, our team and the distributor prioritised demand and ensured the quantities and timelines were met. When we met with the distributor during a review, we learned that the reason for the size and urgency of the order was that there had been a visual data breach at the company. An executive from the company had been travelling and, unknown to him, an executive from one of his competitors was sitting next to him during the journey. He was working with some classified information and all the while his competitor was watching and making notes. I'm not sure how the company discovered the issue, as this information was never disclosed, but the breach became a warning to other companies and executives.

The simple use of a privacy filter would have prevented this serious issue for the company and, to their credit, they acted with urgency, putting in place a new security policy across the entire organisation.

This story of the visual data breach become well known in the industry and the reason that many other companies put similar visual security policies in place. In fact, our team received many enquiries from people who had heard the story and wanted to reduce the risk to their organisation.

Stories can be powerful motivators for customer behaviour.

Why stories matter

So why have I told you this story? At the Solutions Discussion stage of the INSPIRe Secret Sales System, the focus is on positioning your solution to meet your client's needs. This positioning is crucial and will set you apart. Bill Gates once said that 'if you show people the problems and you show people the solutions, they will be moved to act'.[14] This perfectly sums up the next stage of our process. If you connect problems (or needs) with the solutions you can offer, your clients will feel compelled to act. If you can do so with a compelling story or anecdote, you'll captivate your clients in a way that your competition won't be able to match if they're selling using facts and figures. Stories are always more powerful than statistics.

---

14 'Net fuels Live 8 extravaganza' (BBC News, 2005), http://news.bbc. co.uk/1/hi/technology/4648003.stm, accessed 28 September 2020

I hope that as you read the story you started to think about how you could more creatively position your own product or service. This is a great time to capture those thoughts. And you may also want to write down these questions in your journal or notebook and answer them as you work through the chapter:

- What is your story (about you, the company, your product/service)?

- How could you display your uniqueness?

- What is the most interesting and compelling insight you could share?

- How could you weave your knowledge and experience into a fascinating anecdote?

- What would captivate your clients?

- How could you give your clients a true experience of your product or service?

Discuss, don't pitch

At this stage, there's a reason we use the word 'discussion' and not 'pitch'. During your presentation of solutions, it's important to keep checking in with your client. Mediocre salespeople think that 'solutions pitching' comes right after the introduction, and sometimes before. Actually, it doesn't come at all – it's always a discussion.

Reminder: if you don't fully understand your client's needs at this stage, you aren't relevant, and your chances of success will plummet.

Instead of pitching, have a solutions discussion to make sure the client is following what you're saying and that they believe you. If you don't, you risk losing your client along the way. When you choose to have a discussion (rather than to pitch), the conversation flows, even though at this stage you'll likely be doing a lot of the talking. A discussion format allows your client to give you feedback, which you can address immediately. The client won't have to wait until you've finished your presentation to address something that's bothering them. It's a more effective way to alleviate your client's concerns, and you and your client will naturally end up with the right solution to meet your joint needs.

Positioning your solution – features, advantages and benefits

Your organisation will likely have furnished you with the relevant marketing descriptions and a list of the product's/service's key attributes – ie, features. If you don't have these things, I strongly recommend that you either ask your marketing or management team to develop them or invest some time into creating them. The template later in this chapter will give you a framework to do just that. Being clear on your solution's features is fundamental to a successful solutions discussion. Without this knowledge, you won't be consistent or impactful in your client meetings.

When you're positioning your solution (as part of the discussion), it's important to understand the difference between features, advantages and benefits. The differences are subtle but important:

- Feature – what your product/service does

- Advantage – how it's better than other product/service options

- Benefit – the [unique] value your client will get from using your product or service

Some people will naturally consider the advantages or benefits of something (once they understand the features), but not everyone thinks this way. When you're selling a solution that incorporates technology, that is service based or that is complex in any way, always set out the features, advantages and benefits to your client. No exceptions. If you leave it to your client to figure out, you'll risk the impact being diluted, at best, or completely lost. As you explain the features, advantages and benefits, in this order, be enthusiastic to engage and excite your client about the way in which your solution will help them. And of course you can weave in a story or a client referral.

Here's a simple structure to help you remember how to position the features, advantages and benefits consistently:

1. The [insert solution] offers you [insert feature].

2. It's better than [insert other option] because [insert advantage].

3. This means that [insert benefit].

Here's an example:

> The INSPIRe Secret Sales System offers you a simple, powerful and consistent sales process.
>
> It's better than other sales programmes because it's easier to remember, easier to use and easier for sales leaders to coach salespeople in.
>
> This means that you increase team performance, sales results and client satisfaction.

You don't have to use this exact format, but it's a structure to start from. Also, your solution is likely to have multiple features, advantages and benefits, so you can use this structure to lay them out and make sure you cover them comprehensively with your client.

The most powerful piece of this structure is the benefit to your client – you must ensure the benefit is clear and compelling. So how do you know that you've explained your solution's benefits? There's a way to sense-check this.

The 'so what?' rule

The 'so what?' rule is a tried and tested way to confirm that the benefit you're laying out to your client is just that: a true benefit. The rule is simple: the benefit to your client is only a benefit if the question 'so what?' doesn't undermine it.

When you're conceiving benefits, test each one with 'so what?' to make sure you're stating a benefit and not a feature or advantage. As a rule of thumb, a true benefit will do one of the following:

- Deliver the client savings in time or money

- Generate time or money for the client

The saving or generation of time can be linked to the client's needs – ie, they'll have more time to work on their passions, more personal time, more time to generate business, more time to think and plan. And if they're saving or generating money, they can run a more successful business or better reward their team, increase their earnings or generally improve their financial position. If you bear this rule in mind during your solutions discussions, you'll always be relevant to your client.

The solution loop

To show the client that you understand them, loop back to their needs when explaining the features, advantages and benefits of your product or service – you'll create a bespoke solution for your client. It's as simple as adding a line which simply states the client's relevant need. If we added a solution loop to our earlier example, we'd end up with this:

> The INSPIRe Secret Sales System offers you a simple, powerful and consistent sales process.
>
> It's better than other sales programmes because it's easier to remember, easier to use and easier for sales leaders to coach salespeople in.
>
> This means that you increase team performance, sales results and client satisfaction.
>
> You mentioned earlier that improving your sales conversion rates and increasing sales growth were your two highest priorities. This programme will help you achieve both goals.

While this is displayed as a series of statements, remember that your client meeting should be a discussion. Allow the conversation to flow and pay attention to your client's responses. If they're showing positive body language (nodding, smiling or giving you an encouraging look), let them process what you've said.

Link each of the features, advantages and benefits to the needs the client expressed in the Needs Discovery stage of the process. This is critical to gain their acceptance of your solution. Then clarify that they agree the solution you're discussing meets their needs. You can use a closed or open question to do this. For example:

- Do you agree that this will give you what you need?

- What do you think about the solution in principle?

At this stage, you'll likely have gained acceptance. The client should be able to clearly see that your solution will meet their needs. If there are any concerns that haven't yet been raised, this is the point to clarify and deal with them.

I've developed a worksheet I use with clients and teams. It's called the FABSOL worksheet, and it will help you position your solution's features, advantages, benefits and incorporate a solution loop. You can download a copy of the FABSOL template here: https://bit.ly/FABSOL-sheet.

A note about unique selling points

I'm sure you've come across the term 'unique selling point' during your time in sales. I prefer the term 'unique selling benefit'. As we've discussed, it's important to position your solution's benefits appropriately, otherwise the client will think or ask 'so what?'. If your solution has a unique feature, understanding how it will benefit your client is arguably more important than the feature itself!

If your solution does have a unique selling benefit, you'll have a strong advantage over your competition. And now you know how to position that uniqueness in the right way so that your client will appreciate it and you'll be relevant to them.

Sales Mastery: Commit to expertise

Making time for professional development

The longer you work with your clients, the greater their expectations of you will become. That's a good thing. They'll come to see you as a trusted source of information about the market, industry or profession they're in. I encourage you to embrace this expectation and be proactive in your development within your field of expertise. Here are some suggestions:

- Be intentional about developing your expertise

- Read industry/professional publications

- Know the trends and major initiatives in the marketplace

- Identify the opinion leaders and what they're saying (quotes are valuable)

- Understand what's controversial and why

- Know the useful statistics – market growth rates, key challenges, investment decisions, etc.

- Learn about the latest techniques or principles

- Know your competition – what they're saying, current products, key issues they're facing, etc.

- Know the specific unique advantages you have

If you dedicate a set amount of time in your diary to learn about your industry (I suggest thirty minutes a week), within a couple of months, you'll have developed a level of expertise that will astound you. You'll then be more confident in client sales meetings and build your credibility in your organisation and the wider industry in which you work. Professional development will take you far over time.

Reflecting on your questioning

Once you have completed this Solutions Discussion work, you'll likely identify more questions that you need to ask your client to better understand their needs as they relate to your solution. This is a good time to consider the bigger picture. Getting clear on your solution's features, advantages and benefits will have helped you position your solution and link back to your client's needs. Now, it's time to update your HQQs. This isn't about second-guessing your client's needs but helping you meet them more effectively.

I recommend referring to your HQQs bank and updating it – add or amend questions as necessary after reviewing this chapter. I also suggest reviewing your FABSOL Working Table and noting which features, advantages and benefits you should address in your client meetings. These must link to known or unrealised client needs as part of the solutions loop. Finally, review the INSPIRe worksheet, so that you are building a consistent and comprehensive approach.

You've had a comprehensive solutions discussion with your client. You've addressed their needs, clearly laid out the benefits they'll receive from your solution, engaged them with your storytelling and convinced them of your credibility with your expertise, evidence and client referrals. It's time to make a proposal.

Before we move on, reflect on this chapter and write down your thoughts in your journal or notebook.

OPTIONAL EXERCISE: FEATURES, ADVANTAGES AND BENEFITS

Write down a series of features, advantages and benefits your solution offers (using the structure presented in this chapter). Capture how these can be part of a solution loop (back to your client's needs).

Then continue the optional exercise from the previous chapter.

Practise:

- Summarising your clients' needs in their language
- Delivering the features, advantages and benefits of your product/service
- Linking these to your client's needs using the solution loop
- Ensuring that your client is ready for you to make a proposal

11

Proposal Agreement

INSPIRe – Secret Sales System: Proposal Agreement

During my time as a key account manager in a large dental company, I was responsible for a large chain that was an innovator in the corporate dentistry space. I managed to secure a meeting with the procurement director (we'll call him Len) for the group. This first meeting did not go well.

Len was intrigued but went to great lengths to let me know that my organisation was late to the party. The group had been working with other large dental companies for years and had an approved-products list across their chain. The reviews of these approved products were infrequent (every three or so years), and any new product had to be 'worthwhile' for them to make a change. It had been only two years since the last review.

During that meeting, I asked countless questions about the chain – how they worked, their process for selecting suppliers and products, their selection criteria, etc. All Len would say was that cost was the overriding factor; nothing else mattered to them. I felt deflated leaving that meeting. I worked for the most expensive supplier in the market, we had little price flexibility and I knew the competitor sales reps dealing with this account – they were entrenched and good at what they did. This was going to be a long, slow process, if I could even create an opportunity.

I won't go through all the details, but I ended up winning a significant piece of business with this group. It took me a year. Here's the summary of how I did it:

- I used my sales skills and experience.

- I widened my network in the account.

- I identified and built strong rapport with the key decision makers.

- I learned what they needed and what they didn't realise they needed.

- I asked for data about the products they used.

- I analysed that data and learned some interesting facts that they weren't aware of.

- I created a proposal that blew their socks off!

I proposed supplying them with one of the most expensive products in its category available in the market at a discounted rate (as they were the largest end-user purchaser of products in the country) but a rate that was still higher than that of the current supplier. Through my discussions with Len and the data-usage reports I'd reviewed, I learned that while they had an approved-products list, their organisational adherence to that list wasn't good. When I spoke with the key decision makers and users, I found out that they didn't trust some of the approved products and were prepared to face backlash from senior management for noncompliance. Interestingly, the non-approved products were being purchased at full market price. I made some rudimentary calculations about how much extra they were paying across the product category (which included some of my company's products) and learned that the discount I needed to propose was lower than I'd expected.

The other interesting factor was the response from my organisation's senior management team. They hadn't been asked to consider a single proposal of this size before (we hadn't dealt with clients like this centrally), and they hadn't been presented with an opportunity of this magnitude either. We were on new ground. And that didn't make things any easier. The negotiations within my organisation weren't straightforward, and this work was almost as difficult as the work I was doing with my client. I decided it could be useful to explain this to Len.

I was as transparent as I could be with him, explaining that the internal sign-off for a proposal of this size would take a lot of persuasion and time on my behalf but that I was committed to creating a viable and valuable proposal for him and working hard behind the scenes to make it happen. Len seemed to appreciate this, and on many occasions during the months of negotiations and discussions he'd ask how I was getting on with my 'internal selling'. He thanked me for my continued efforts.

The final proposal I developed (with the valuable help of my management team) laid out several factors that the competition and my client hadn't considered before:

- The savings that could be made through standardisation

- The value of training and education across their practices to deliver standardisation (and generate accredited continuing professional development hours)

- The improved buy-in from their organisation as a result of using a 'trusted' brand

- The potential cost of poor-quality products and the subsequent impact on the client's reputation, future brand, employee engagement and patient attraction and retention

- The opportunity to collaborate with an industry leader, beyond just product supply

I remember when Len called to tell me that our proposal had been accepted and we were going to be added to the approved-product list. I was thrilled that my hard work had paid off. The experience taught me a valuable lesson in strategic account selling, and it paid off many times in the future. I went on to lead teams who were selling to and managing large, complex accounts with long sales cycles. Money can't buy this kind of experience.

Checking in with the client

Once you've reached Proposal Agreement in the sales system, you're coming to the closing stages of your client meeting. If you've followed the INSPIRe Secret Sales System correctly, you and your client will be looking to confirm details and move forward. This is the point at which you should make a proposal – in other words, close the sale. I prefer the phrase 'proposal agreement' as it signals to you that this is the time to make a proposal and that the aim is to gain the client's agreement to that proposal. 'Closing the sale' can have negative connotations. It might conjure images of the salesperson putting pressure on the client. That's sometimes appropriate, but you should always aim for agreement. Agreement builds the foundation for a strong, positive, long-term relationship with your client.

Before making your proposal, check in with the client by asking a simple question. For example:

- Is there anything else we need to cover before we move on to discussing the final proposal?

- I'd just like to check that what we've discussed meets your needs and that you're ready for me to make a proposal. Would that be OK?

- If we move forward and I make a proposal, do you have everything you need to make a decision?

These types of questions will enable your client to either agree to move forward, seek clarification on items they're uncertain about or raise an objection. If they confirm their agreement, you move to the next stage of the system (which we'll look at next). If they're seeking clarification, address any questions or reservations. And if they raise an objection, you must work through the relevant steps to resolve it.

Handling objections

Nobody is perfect! There will likely be times when you find yourself close to the end of the sale, close to gaining a commitment, and suddenly your client throws in an objection, taking the wind out of your sails. Sound familiar?

The best way to approach objections is to remind yourself of the INSPIRe Secret Sales System. Return to the Needs Discovery stage. Remember, the process moves in both directions between Proposal Agreement, Solutions Discussion and Needs Discovery. An objection means your client has an unmet need. It's useful to consider that an objection is a signal that the client is seriously considering your proposal. See it as a positive signal.

Selling sometimes involves dealing with egos. You might have a client who's downright awkward and will make statements that seem contrary just for the sake of it. We've all met these people. Before a client meeting, one of the best things you can do is consciously 'park your ego at the front door'. I recommend picturing yourself actually doing this. It can be a calming part of your meeting preparation. It's easy to get drawn into arguments with difficult clients, and before you know it, you'll find yourself in a tit-for-tat debate that you cannot win (if you win the argument, you lose the client!). In these situations, remember: the only thing that matters is meeting your client's needs and winning the business. You don't need to win an argument, and you certainly don't need to prove that you're right.

If you're faced with a client who is clearly in the wrong but won't be told otherwise – perhaps they're making incorrect statements about the marketplace or other clients – there's a simple and effective way to handle the situation:

- Don't agree or disagree with them (agreeing can reinforce their point while disagreeing can cause an argument).

- Acknowledge and understand their perspective.

- Stay neutral on the topic; remain objective.

- Allow your client to vent (often that's all they want). Ask only light questions.

- Link back to their needs and return to the INSPIRe Secret Sales System.

This simple, effective approach will help you enormously with difficult clients.

Objections will vary, but generally they fall into one of three categories:

- Misunderstanding

- Scepticism

- Genuine needs objection

Let's walk through them and look at the ways you can handle each one.

Misunderstanding

A misunderstanding happens when your client doesn't fully understand the way in which your solution works. It's fairly common for people to raise objections based on a misunderstanding. The best way to handle a misunderstanding is to take these steps:

- Empathise, and then clarify the misunderstanding: 'What exactly is the concern?'

- Listen to, understand and summarise the objection.

- Apologise for the fact that *you* weren't clear the first time around.

- Explain that you may have caused a misunderstanding and clarify that your solution will deliver what your client needs.

- Confirm that the misunderstanding has been addressed.

This is the most straightforward objection to resolve. Once your client confirms it has been addressed, you can move forward.

Scepticism

Scepticism is when your client doesn't believe that your solution is able to do what you're saying it will do. To put it another way, 'It's too good to be true!' When someone displays scepticism, it's easy to become dismissive and defend your position forcefully. This will only make your client more sceptical. The best way to address scepticism is to be prepared for it. This is where evidence, demonstrations and statements from other clients about how well your solution works are highly valuable. The following steps will help you to address scepticism:

- Empathise, and then clarify the scepticism: 'What exactly is the concern?'

- Listen to, understand and summarise the objection.

- Ask what evidence the client would like to see to give them confidence that your solution will deliver what they need.

- If your client isn't able to tell you what would convince them, consider:

    - A practical demonstration (if possible)

- Showing client testimonials

- Offering to share contact details of a similar (current) satisfied client

- Presenting evidence and case studies

- Offering a trial or evaluation (if possible)

Scepticism can slow down your sales cycle but must be addressed fully or your client could become a wider issue for your business; if you can't convince them, they may become vocal about it to other potential clients. Take the time needed to convince them. Be patient and find out what it will take to prove to your client that your solution will do what you say it will do. Scepticism presents you with an opportunity – your client could become a significant advocate once you've convinced them. Imagine your client saying, 'Well I didn't believe it at first, but the solution did everything I was told it would!' Successfully address their scepticism, and this is a probable outcome.

You also have an opportunity to negotiate here. Make your client a proposition. For example: 'So if I prove to you that our solution delivers, will you agree to write me a testimonial?' This might be a fair trade – a free trial for an evaluation of your service. And delivered in the right way, this type of negotiation can further strengthen your client relationship.

Genuine needs objection

This is the trickiest objection of them all. A client will make a genuine needs objection when your solution will meet some but not all their needs. The best way to handle this situation is to take these steps:

- Empathise, and then clarify the genuine needs objection: 'What exactly is the concern?'

- Listen to, understand and summarise the objection.

- Be honest about the mismatch between your client's needs and your solution.

- Highlight the needs your client has that your solution *does* meet.

- Ask your client to prioritise their needs: 'Which is most important?'

- Consider what you could do to minimise your solution's shortfall.

- Ask your client, 'What would it take for you to choose my solution?'

If your client decides that your solution isn't right for them after you've taken these steps, you may have to accept it. The final thing you can do is ask your client to sleep on it and agree on a time to have a follow-up discussion. As you wrap up the meeting, remind the client of the needs your solution does meet and let them know you genuinely hope you can work together. Before your follow-up discussion, speak with other clients who may have had the same objection and overcome it (ask around your company). You can then send a message to your client with the additional information or wait until your follow-up discussion to give them the new facts you've discovered. This may get you back in the game. If not, remember, you can't please everyone.

The more objections you handle, the better you'll get at it. And objections can really help with client loyalty. If you have to work hard to make the sale, the client may be someone who is hard to please, more difficult for other salespeople to convert and more loyal to you because you made the effort to go the extra mile to satisfy them.

The proposal

Making your proposal should be a straightforward task at this point. Be confident, clear and concise. You've worked hard to get here and have earned the right to make a bold proposal that meets your client's needs. Make sure your language is concise and assertive. Don't pose your proposal as a question – it's a statement and it's tailored to your client, so be proud to make it.

Your proposal should be comprehensive and cover all the aspects of your solution. If it would help to have a template as a reminder of these aspects, this is the time to complete it and share it with your client. In some instances, depending on the complexity of your offering, you may work through the proposal with your client and fill in a template as you go along.

I'm a big fan of templates, or order forms. They help you and your client to be clear on exactly what's being agreed to and give you the chance to get the optimal order size and include any optional extras or additional service agreements. If you don't work with templates and you'd like to, I suggest speaking with your line manager or marketing department and developing something that works for you. You may even be able to develop a web-based order form that will allow your client to immediately place an order. It's a great way to show how efficient your organisation is and will give your client confidence in their decision.

Depending on your business, the proposal may need to be sent to the client after the meeting, either by email or in the post (or both). You may need sign-off from a line manager, depending on the size or complexity of the proposal, or you may work in a regulated industry, in which case you'll need to have documentation approved. In any case, I suggest you work through all the details with the client and explain what they can expect to receive. You don't want them to experience any unwanted surprises. They will appreciate this clarity.

Your proposal may include some or all of the following:

- The stages of your service offering (if a repeat purchase)

- Quantity / volumes

- Pricing / value

- Timing

- Payment options and terms

- Purchase route

- Additional accessories / supplements

Once you've reviewed the proposal, you've handled any and all objections with grace and your client is in agreement, it's time to do a final check to make sure everything meets with the client's approval. Once you've done this, you and the client will reach agreement on the immediate action. We'll cover that in the next chapter.

Sales Mastery: Proposal negotiation

Using a framework

When you're making a proposal, it's easy to feel as though the hard work is done. You may want to just get it over with and move on. But remember, this is an important moment for your client. They're making an investment in you, so don't rush the process. Focus on making the experience positive for your client, from start to finish.

For some clients, negotiation is a part of the proposal process – they will always believe they can get a better deal. Your job is to help them realise that your proposal is the best deal possible. If your organisation doesn't have a framework in place for managing negotiations (ie, a discount structure linked to your client's commitment to volume, term, value, etc.), I suggest you request that one be created by your company's management team. There are several reasons why you should work from a structured framework for discounting. Here are a few:

- It gives you, your organisation and your clients a consistent pricing structure.

- It creates parity, equality and fairness for your clients and your marketplace.

- It enables you to objectively recognise client commitment.

- It's beneficial for both you and your client if structured correctly.

- It creates transparency in the event of an audit or inspection.

Here's a good rule of thumb: if you make a statement, comment or put something down in writing, you should be prepared for that information to be published on the front page of a major newspaper (with your name on it)! If you're not prepared for that, don't communicate the information in any way. The same principle applies to your discounting framework. You need to have a structure that you could justify if it were shared across your client base. A structure that is open, transparent and fair will give you and your client greater confidence and build trust.

You or your organisation will need to consider *in advance* what's desired (what's of value) in exchange for a discount. This list isn't exhaustive, but it should give you some ideas:

- Shorter payment terms or payment upfront

- A written recommendation

- A case-study document or video

- A referral to another client

- A longer contract term

- A higher volume commitment

- Regular order patterns

- A single order with central delivery

- A tiered service or product offering

It's important to take these two key factors into account when discounting:

- Any discount given to your client will impact your sales figures by reducing the value of the sale.

- Discounting will impact the company's profitability, and the organisation may need to adjust sales commissions or bonuses.

If you're able to offer discounts on price or show flexibility on aspects of your solution and understand the impact these things will have on your business, you have some negotiating leverage.

Through negotiating courses I've taken over the years, I've learned several useful techniques. Let's look at the most relevant ones.

The professional flinch

The professional flinch is exactly what it sounds like – a flinch that you've practised and then carry out whenever you receive a request that you'll find difficult to honour or that you don't want to or can't meet.

The best way to go about it is to pretend that you're in pain – as if someone has physically hurt you. You recoil, scrunch up your face and squint as you draw air through your teeth. Think about watching a video of someone slipping on ice and landing hard. You'll likely flinch. This is the reaction we're looking for.

After you flinch, wait in silence. The other person will feel intense pressure, and you'll then be in a strong position during negotiation discussions. You can use the professional flinch whenever you feel that un-reasonable demands are being made on you or that someone is behaving in a way that you don't think is right. Watch how powerful it is.

'If you... then I...'

In a negotiation, it's fundamental not to give some-thing without asking for something. Consider what you want in return for making a concession. The recommended phrase in this situation is 'If you... then I...' Get comfortable using it. It *will* enable you to negotiate more effectively.

Here's an example. Imagine your client is asking for a 5% discount on your proposal and you're able to meet this request but would like them to commit to a longer term. You might say something like this:

'Well, the proposal I've made gives you access to our best pricing. However, *if you* are prepared to extend the contract to a full year, instead of six months, *then* *I* would be able to give you a 5% discount.'

This will put you in the driving seat and give you control of the negotiation. Silence comes into play again here as well (see Chapter 9 for a recap on silence). After you've made your negotiating statement, be silent and wait for your client's response. In a negotiation, the first person to speak following a proposal is more likely to accept the other person's proposal. Throughout a negotiation there may be several statements made and positions taken. This is good, as it shows progress. Make sure you continue to use the phrase 'If you, then I...'.

Price anchoring

When discussing pricing with your client in a negotiation, it's important to 'anchor' your price. This simply means stating your price over and over. By doing this, you start to condition your client to your price and not the price they've requested or stated. Even if you offer a discount, refer to your starting price. At an unconscious level this gives you control in the negotiation.

Just as your proposal should be stated clearly and assertively, so should your price. It's a statement, not a question – be confident and direct. This sets you up to anchor your price during any negotiation. If your client raises a challenge, you can say or ask something along these lines:

- £1,203 [whatever the price is] provides excellent value for the quality and service we discussed.

- How close to £1,203 can you get?

- So, in principle, you could commit to the price of £1,203 if I could make a X% discount.

There are many ways in which you can anchor your price. The key is remembering to do so – don't be drawn into referencing your client's price request. Keeping the discussion focused on your price keeps the balance of power in your favour.

Defer to a higher power

Sometimes your client may make a request that is beyond your level of authority or makes you uncomfortable. Remember, it's just a request. The best way to handle these situations is to defer to a higher power. In other words, explain that you aren't able to make that decision and you'll have to gain approval. At this stage, if you don't think you can meet the client's request, tell them. But if you believe you can gain approval, this is an opportunity to delight your client. The client will feel in control, and it will also strengthen your hand in the negotiation. Deferring to a higher power allows you to buy time, shows your commitment, relieves pressure for both parties and can get your client firmly on your side. Creating space in these situations allows your client time to reflect, which could lead to them reconsidering their position. Make sure you know your client's deadlines so that you get back to them in good time and don't undermine the good work you've done so far with a delayed response.

In these circumstances, you are well within your rights to make a greater demand of your client. If you're preparing to ask your manager for an additional discount or service, you need to be able to take something away in exchange. Many salespeople in this position simply 'give away' a discount or service without asking for anything in return. From this point on, make a commitment to knowing what you want and making the request of your client in exchange for meeting their demands.

In your journal or notebook, write down a list of ideas for negotiation requests you could make of your clients. With this list you'll be forearmed. And as we learned in Chapter 4, preparation gives you greater confidence, control and power in your client meetings.

There are many resources on negotiation available. If you want to become more proficient, I suggest doing further research. One particularly good book is *Never Split the Difference*, by Chris Voss and Tahl Raz.[15] It's an original look at negotiations, seen through the lens of hostage negotiations. It's a compelling read littered

---

15 C Voss and T Raz, *Never Split the Difference: Negotiating as if your life depended on it* (Random House, 2017)

with stories and anecdotes that offer practical principles for effective negotiations.

Take some time to review your worksheet and make
note of the key components that should be included in
your proposals as part of your client meetings. These
can be headlines, criteria or negotiating points. This
will further strengthen your personalised INSPIRe
Secret Sales System.

Before we move on, reflect on this chapter and write
down your thoughts in your journal or notebook.

OPTIONAL EXERCISE: THE PROPOSAL

Continue the optional exercise from the previous
chapter.

Practise:

- Ensuring that your client is ready for you to make a
  proposal
- Delivering a confident, concise and compelling
  proposal
- Handling the objections your client raises using the
  structure in this chapter
- Clarifying that your client is satisfied that their
  objections have been addressed

12

Immediate Action

INSPIRe – Secret Sales System: Immediate Action

When I worked as a medical sales manager, one part of our business was selling wound-care products to district nursing teams. Selling to these teams was both rewarding and frustrating. There was a process that needed to be followed to get our products included as part of the wider customer organisation's product formulary (their recommended-product list). Then there was the challenge of actually getting the nursing teams to use the products once they were on the list. Not all the district nurses were aware of the list or followed it, so generating sales was complex and time-consuming. Some members of my team had gained significant formulary inclusions but weren't realising the sales benefit.

Because district nurses treat patients in their own homes, they can be difficult to pin down, but they do return to their base (usually a GP surgery or health centre) at lunch to update notes, refill medical stock, meet with colleagues and attend supplier training sessions. The team could get meetings at lunch, but the nurses were busy, often distracted and keen to get going for their afternoon shifts. It was important to make those meetings as effective as possible.

We used the principles of the INSPIRe Secret Sales System to engage the district nursing teams, to understand and meet their needs and to show them how our products were the best to meet their needs and their patients'. The final piece of the puzzle that enabled the team to realise their sales results was agreement on the immediate action that the district nurse and my team would take, either during or following the meeting. This was a critical step in gaining commitment.

Once the district nurse agreed that they would use our product on their patients, the team would ask the nurse to do the following:

- Identify and confirm the *first patient* on which they would use the product.

- Confirm the date and time they were seeing the patient.

- Explain what improvement they thought the patient would experience [this was important, as it confirmed they understood *why* they were choosing to use our product].

- Confirm the best time [after that patient visit] for a check-in.

- Agree on a time to review and discuss their progress.

When the team started to use this approach, their sales improved notably. The process took time, but the positive impact was clear. Immediate Action is a critical phase in the sales process.

Getting commitment

You could be forgiven for thinking that at this stage of the sales process, the deal is done and you can punch the air or high-five the receptionist on the way out of the building (neither of which you should do, by the way, just so we're clear). But it's vital to make and gain a commitment. This is what the Immediate Action phase is all about. It's the obligation that ensures what you've discussed with your client actually happens. Without this final stage, you'll find that 'stuff' gets in the way of your client moving forward with what you've agreed in your meeting. Trust me, it just does.

Once you leave your client's office, their life goes on, the emails flood in, the office door gets knocked on, their partner calls, they have a crisis to deal with or a fire to put out – any number of things will throw them off course. It's not personal. In today's busy world, if you don't get your client to commit to taking immediate action, there's a high risk that what you've agreed on won't happen. Getting things right at this stage will give your sales results and client meetings a significant boost.

You may feel like you're overdoing it at this point, perhaps creating a 'hard sell' situation. But you're not. Having gotten this far with your client – you've identified that they have a real need, you have a solution, and you and the client agree that the proposal is mutually beneficial – you owe it to them to complete the sale successfully. That means making sure that you both follow through on the actions required to complete the transaction or finalise commitment to the proposal.

It's an appropriate time to be absolutely clear that you're confirming the proposal and the corresponding actions. I suggest asking a simple assumptive question in a conversational style. Something similar to the following:

- So are you happy if we go ahead with the proposal?

- Is there anything else we need to consider before we go ahead and confirm the proposal?

- If we were to confirm today, would there be any other information you'd need?

This final check allows your client to agree and allows you to progress. Be silent and listen. If the client has any reservations, remember INSPIRe and work back through their needs, your solution and any objections. And if necessary, adjust your proposal. It's as simple as that.

Once you have agreement, summarise what has been agreed and confirm the actions that must be taken to finalise the transaction and ensure the deal goes ahead.

At this stage, you and the client should agree to:

- The actions you will take to process the order (and the timing of those actions)

- The actions your client will take (and the timing of those actions)

- The next steps (implementation or product/ service training)

- Who else will need to be involved and who will follow up with them, and when

- A date and time for a follow-up discussion (to make sure everything is to your client's satisfaction)

- A review date (a more formal review of business)

A plan that outlines who will do what by when produces clarity and ensures commitment. If you haven't been completing this final stage in your sales interactions and start doing so now, you'll likely notice that the rate at which your clients go from simply saying they'll do something (and then you have to chase them) to actually doing what you've both agreed will increase dramatically.

Sales Mastery: The power of feedback and gratitude

Feedback

Surprisingly, few salespeople ask for feedback at the end of a client meeting. Most want to get out quickly, celebrate the win (or commiserate the loss) and move on to the next big thing. But if you make a point of asking for feedback at the end of every client meeting, you'll learn what really works for your client and what you need to do to make yourself and your organisation even better in the future.

You might not get feedback every time – if your clients aren't used to being asked for feedback, they may not be able to think of anything. But if your client cannot think of any concrete feedback, they're likely to say that they're satisfied with the meeting, or the outcome of it. This in itself is a powerful positive reinforcement for your client. They have confirmed for themselves, out loud (which further reinforces their point of view), that you've met their needs and they wouldn't change anything.

When asking for feedback, do so with two simple questions:

> Before we finish today, I wonder if I could ask for your feedback on this meeting. How did you find it?

Listen, be silent and take the feedback on board (make a note). Follow up with:

> What would you change?

Once again listen, be silent and take the feedback on board (make a note).

Always thank your client for their feedback. You may also need to respond to the feedback directly.

The final thank you

After every client meeting, take the time to genuinely appreciate your client. They have the freedom to spend their time how they wish and choose any of the suppliers in the marketplace. And they have chosen *you*! Think about it for a moment – this is a significant compliment. Recognise it and declare it to your client. Expressing your sincere thanks and appreciation for their time, and their trust in you to satisfy their business needs, is the perfect way to show your client how much you value them. It will make them feel justified in their choice, it will reinforce your relationship and it will strengthen the loyalty your client shows you.

If you can generate a positive emotion in your client when you end a meeting with them, this will be their lasting memory of the meeting. Appreciation is incredibly powerful. Sincere gratitude can create real warmth in a relationship, so grant this to your client at the end of every meeting. Then, every time your client uses your product or service, they'll think of you, and every time they think of you, they'll think about how well you listen, how you genuinely meet their needs and how you're grateful for their business. This creates a positive cycle in your client's mind and emotional centre that will cement your relationship with them beyond the solution or even the organisation. *You* win their heart!

Take some time to review your worksheet and make note of how to incorporate immediate action into your client meetings to bolster your personalised INSPIRe Secret Sales System.

Before we move on, reflect on this chapter and write down your thoughts in your journal or notebook.

OPTIONAL EXERCISE: TAKING ACTION

Continue the optional exercise from the previous chapter.

Practise:

- Finalising the list of actions you and your client will take
- Agreeing on the check-in time
- Agreeing on the review date
- Asking for feedback
- Expressing your thanks and appreciation

13

Reflection (Self-coaching)

INSPIRe – Secret Sales System: Reflection

When I was working as a sales representative in 2002, I covered a lot of miles in my car. I'd while away the time listening to the radio and calling my colleagues. One weekend, I visited my mother-in-law, Pam, with my wife and children. Pam had just completed an MSc in Health Management and was working as a manager in the NHS. She had a good career and had been interested in her professional development for some years. I talked to her about my career aspirations and Pam told me that she had a couple of books I might be interested in reading – they had helped in her development: *Unlimited Power*, by Anthony Robbins,[16] and *Learned Optimism*, by Martin Seligman.[17]

She also asked me if I'd seen Tony Robbins in action. At that stage, I hadn't. She loaded a video on her computer then said, 'I've seen it before. I'll leave you to it.' I watched in awe. Tony Robbins' ability to connect with people and help them transform their lives seemed effortless.

That was a significant day in my life. I committed to my personal and professional development. I started buying (and, this is crucial, actually reading and listening to) books and audio programmes about self-development, sales, business, high performance and personal success. I realised that to generate the level of success I wanted in my life, I simply had to learn the necessary skills. I also realised that I had a significant amount of time at my disposal – time that I was

---

16   A Robbins, *Unlimited Power: The new science of personal achievement* (Pocket Books, 2001)

17   M Seligman, *Learned Optimism: How to change your mind and your life* (Free Press, 2002)

currently spending listening to the radio and making non-essential phone calls. I worked out what I wanted for my career and then went about reading the books and listening to programmes by the best in the field. Once I gained the knowledge, I implemented what I learned. I got so much better at my job, I enjoyed it more and my career took off.

I took the approach of improving myself to improve my career. During my time as a salesperson, key account manager, sales manager and business leader, I focused on the incremental improvements I could make each day. It's incredible how much you can improve over the course of a year, broken down into months and weeks. The self-development and personal growth gives you confidence, and it helps you realise that you can achieve any goal you set for yourself over time. There are so many examples of people who have harnessed the power of reflection to stimulate their development and transform their lives.

Making big change with small steps

In the introduction to this book I referenced *The Greatest Salesman in the World*, by Og Mandino.[18] Mandino is a perfect example of the power of self-reflection. In his mid-thirties, having served in the military, he found himself jobless and addicted to alcohol. Dur-

---

18   O Mandino, *The Greatest Salesman in the World* (Jaico Publishing House, 2008)

ing a harsh winter, he sought shelter in a library and started reading books about personal development. These books and his subsequent actions changed his life. He became one of the most widely read self-help authors ever. Before his death, at the age of seventy-two, he'd become one of the most sought-after public speakers in the world.[19]

While his is an incredible story, it's not entirely unique. The number of people who are able to turn their lives around by committing to self-development is inspiring. There's genuinely no telling where your commitment to developing yourself could lead. Make incremental improvements to yourself and your skills every day, and the results will be exponential.

Reflection is an integral part of the INSPIRe Secret Sales System – it's fundamental to your improvement, development and success. Invest time in yourself after every sales call. It's worth it. Regardless of the outcome of a client meeting, take time to reflect on how the meeting went and on your performance in the meeting. Doing so is the simplest and easiest way to dramatically improve your results and stay ahead of your competition.

Here's a simple, fast and effective three-stage reflection practice:

---

19 'About Og Mandino' (Og Mandino Leadership Institute, no date), www.ogmandino.com/about-og-mandino, accessed 28 September 2020

1. Work through self-coaching questions

2. Identify successes and opportunities

3. Commit to improving

Let's walk through these one at a time.

Work through self-coaching questions

High-performing athletes work with a coach, and the same goes for high-performing businesspeople. But if you don't have the luxury of working with a professional coach, you can get into the habit of improving yourself through self-coaching. If you ask yourself these three powerful questions regularly, you'll enhance your performance (I refer to this as the WIN, LEARN, CHANGE model):

1. What are the three key things that went really well? (WIN)

2. What did I learn? (LEARN)

3. What will I change? (CHANGE)

Ask yourself (and answer) these questions after each of your sales interactions.

Identify successes and opportunities

It's important to celebrate your successes. By identifying what has gone well, you create positive momentum for your development. This activity is about becoming consciously aware of and reinforcing what's working for you. Take note of how well you're performing and how much you improve moving forward. When you reinforce what has gone well, your mind is open to learning more. Through learning, you can generate a natural curiosity and greater openness to change. By regularly reflecting and noting the actions you need to take, you can build powerful momentum and your professional development accelerates.

Commit to improving

Finally, commit to maintaining your high performance while also identifying an area that you'll improve upon. This reflection practice is simple and incredibly impactful when repeated regularly. The answers to the questions will create a valuable foundation for your development.

Use this book to guide your development. Revisit the sections and chapters that deliver the most value to you. Consider your development an ongoing process. I like to think of it as committing to lifelong learning. If you choose to, you'll see that there's a lesson in every day, in every interaction and in every person – you just need to look for it. Be open and receptive.

Sales Mastery: Creative self-coaching

A new perspective

Over time, you may find that your self-coaching 'dries up' and you're struggling to find areas for improvement. The best way to overcome this is to work on your self-coaching creativity. Think about self-assessment in different ways. Below are several self-coaching questions that will help you gain new perspectives:

- What would my mentor (or a leader in this field) recommend I focus on?

- If I were 'the greatest salesperson in the world', what would I be doing differently?

- If I had the power of mind control, how would it improve my selling?

- What would I do in my client meetings if I knew I couldn't fail and was guaranteed success?

- If I were capable of anything, what would I do?

Include the answers to these questions in your self-coaching practice to stimulate your creativity and maintain your forward movement and development.

Unlocking your creative self-coaching genius

Within your mind is a genius that can answer any question you ask – you just need to set it free. You're only limited by your imagination. The more you practise asking and answering creative questions, the better you'll get. Here are some more examples of imaginative questions to ask yourself:

- How can I become the best at what I do while creating the most enjoyment for my client and me?

- What is the most fun I can have in my work?

- Who would I have to become to be the person my client thinks of before anyone else?

- How can I transform myself and become the most inspirational person my client knows?

- What could I do that would make me the happiest salesperson on the planet?

- How could I learn to love my profession and my clients more than anything in the world?

- If I loved what I did so much that it no longer felt like work, what would I have to do?

- What is the most courageous action I could take to inspire my clients and me?

- How could I create so much value for my clients that they felt compelled to show their gratitude forever?

This is only a sample of the questions that you could ask yourself – there is no limit! Taking the opportunity to improve and develop yourself and appreciate and enjoy your clients and your work will set you on a journey that lifts your performance and liberates you. After all, nobody can take away the things you learn and the person you become.

I've developed a self-coaching guide to help you in this journey. You can download a copy of the guide here: https://bit.ly/Self-Coach.

The power of reflection

Self-reflection will stimulate and open up your creative mind. You'll take the time to search for answers and have a strong desire to improve and grow. Once you build the habit of self-reflection, your search for answers will expand beyond developing your sales talents. If you can harness the power of self-reflection, it will enable continual positive transformation that will impact every part of your life. Self-reflection will become a cornerstone of your development and success in work and life.

Take some time to review your worksheet and make note of the key components of this chapter that you'd like to include in your personalised INSPIRe Secret Sales System.

Before we move on, reflect on this chapter and write down your thoughts in your journal or notebook.

PART FOUR

LOOKING AHEAD

14

Remote Sales and Influence

Since the COVID-19 pandemic and its resulting lockdowns, companies and leaders have been exploring different working environments and making changes to their business models, working practices and expectations of their teams. During the lockdowns, demand for in-person training and coaching dropped, but the need for virtual / remote training, mentoring and coaching soared.

Salespeople must be able to sell virtually and remotely. As a sales trainer, mentor and coach, I worked with clients during the pandemic to help their teams and leaders learn the optimal way to sell and influence in virtual settings. While much remains the same with remote selling (we mustn't throw the baby out with the bathwater), there are many nuances and adjustments that can make a significant positive impact and give us a distinct competitive advantage.

Here are my top ten principles for mastering remote sales and influence:

1. **Remember and follow your proven sales process.** For us, this is Prepare2 INSPIRe. Prepare for your interactions as usual. Prime yourself and your client. Recap and follow your proven model.

2. **Ensure your hook is powerful (or risk cancellation).** In the new remote world, your clients are busier than ever, so you must make the reason for meeting more compelling than ever. They're trading their time for time with you. Make it count. Spend time crafting a client-centred hook.

3. **Send an agenda and invitation with a compelling heading (your hook).** Once you have a client meeting confirmed, send them an electronic diary invitation. Incorporate your hook into the subject heading. Then send them a reminder the day before, restating the reason why you're meeting. This minimises the risk of a last-minute cancellation.

4. **Use your video, even if they don't.** Wherever possible, get your client on video. Use the opportunity to read body language. I have a client who converts every phone call on his

mobile to a FaceTime call - it's genius and strengthens his relationships. If your client doesn't use video, turn yours on anyway. This way, at least they can see and experience the full you. I've been teaching clients this for years now:

- An email is better than no contact.

- A phone call is better than an email.

- A video call is better than a phone call.

- An in-person meeting is better than a video call.

5. **Turn off all notifications and practise using the platform beforehand.** Before the meeting, turn off anything that could make noise or cause an interruption. Then practise what you're going to say so you're confident and competent. Get comfortable with video calling - contact friends, family and colleagues. Seeing your own image alongside your client's can take some getting used to. Do it in advance of an important call.

6. **Arrive early and set the tone.** Your client is likely to see this as your domain, so you need to control the setting. Arrive early, welcome them, drive the agenda and the meeting: act as the ideal host. If you don't, it will feel strange for both of you and your ability to influence will be seriously diminished.

7. **Look at the camera, not their image.** Lots of people make the mistake of looking at the image of the other person. This means they're not

making eye contact. You must look at the camera to make eye contact with the other person. Your eye will be drawn to your image or theirs, so this takes practice. Invest the time you need to get this right and you'll stand out from your competition.

8. **Get them engaged, interested and involved.** Remember the importance of rapport in client relationships. It's even more important virtually. Make sure you engage and connect before you start selling or your attempts will fall flat.

9. **Listen carefully and pause to allow for the overlap.** On video calls there's often a time lag, so if you're not careful, you'll trip over your client's words. Listening is key. Allow time for your client's answers. Pause for two seconds after your client finishes talking and you'll avoid the issue and create space for both you and your client to think and reflect.

10. **Summarise and confirm actions and next steps.** Clarity is power! At the end of the meeting, summarise key points, check for completeness, confirm actions for both parties, outline next steps and get the next interaction booked in the diary. This way, you'll avoid one of the most common pitfalls for salespeople: chasing clients to follow up after a meeting.

These ten principles have been tried and tested by my clients and their teams. As an addition to the INSPIRe

Secret Sales System, they create significant positive impact for you and your clients.

There's a webinar available as part of an online Sales Mastery programme. You can find the webinar here: https://bit.ly/Webinar-Remote-Sales-June2020.

You can also download my 'Top 10 Principles and Practices for Virtual/Remote Selling' here: https://bit.ly/Remote-Sales-Top10.

Reflect on this chapter and write down your thoughts in your journal or notebook.

15

Future Success

In 2010, I was leading an IT accessories business for a large company. Shortly after taking on the role of business manager, one of our critical salespeople was promoted into another position. After interviewing tens of candidates, I hired a highly experienced salesperson who had worked in the IT sector for many years (let's call him Derek). Derek was a real professional – he knew the marketplace, the client base, the channel and how to sell effectively. I worked with Derek regularly to coach and support him in his role and his development. He settled in quickly and was soon making a positive impact on the business. We liked working together, and Derek was open to coaching, development and continually improving himself. It made the time we spent together valuable and enjoyable for both of us.

One day, Derek was set to conduct a reseller floor walk. This was an opportunity for suppliers of IT equipment and accessories to work with our channel-reseller sales teams to train, troubleshoot and gain 'mindshare' (a term often used in channel relationships – getting your channel partner's sales team to remember your products when speaking with their end-user clients). Derek and I met at the start of the day to set objectives and prepare. When I asked Derek what the plan was, he mentioned that this client had seen an increase in their sales of our products in the last quarter. He was keen to build momentum and I agreed that this would be a valuable use of our time.

We discussed the way in which we'd work throughout the day, and Derek shared that we'd be unlikely to see everyone in one visit simply because of the sheer number of salespeople. I asked Derek about how he prioritised his time. Specifically, I asked, 'Which members of the sales team are driving the growth?'

'Well', he replied, 'I get sent a monthly sales report and that has information about their sales teams' performance.'

I asked him to tell me more about the report. He explained that it contained information such as the names of the salespeople responsible for making sales to the account. When I asked him how he used those names, he replied, 'Well, when I'm with the sales team, I ask how they're getting on selling our products, and if they tell me they've made a sale, then I cross-reference with the list and we discuss it.'

Derek had in his possession important information that could help him prioritise and identify his high-est-potential clients and product advocates, and he wasn't using it!

Because one of Derek's strengths was his coachability and openness to new ideas, I suggested to him that we structure the day with a focus on generating the maximum impact with our time. Despite his open-ness, he gave me a sceptical look. After discussing, we concluded that investing thirty minutes reviewing the sales report, sorting the information to determine which members of the sales team had made the larg-est sales in the previous month and then using that to identify which members of the team we should priori-tise spending time with would be the best course of action. We agreed to seek out the specific salespeople (his clients, in this situation) and thank them for their contribution, ask how they had come about the sale and then discuss additional opportunities we could support them with. This was a change to Derek's usual approach, but doing so would ensure we were spending time with the highest-potential salespeople.

Derek then asked, 'So next time I visit, do you think I should prioritise spending time with the people I don't talk to today? That way, I'll see the whole sales team.' Derek had bought into the principles of prioritisation, but his old patterns and habits were kicking in. He believed that he should be spending time with all the salespeople. We discussed this at length. I explained that the next time he visited (next month), there would be a fresh sales report and different salespeople to prioritise – again, he wouldn't have the time to cover the entire team. I sensed resistance from him, but we agreed to run the day as we'd planned and then review.

The day went incredibly well. All the salespeople were receptive to Derek and me, and we identified the most sales leads Derek had created with a client in a single day. When we reviewed at the end of the day, Derek said to me, 'It was a good decision to prioritise the sales team. This was one of the best floor walks I've had in a while.'

We came away from that day with several principles:

- Reviewing relevant client data is fundamental to effective planning

- Not all clients are created equal

- By spending time with the right clients (prioritising them), the business will grow faster

- Openness to new ways of working will improve sales performance

Derek had a series of successful years in sales. His performance went from strength to strength and his delivery of the client floor walks and meetings continually improved.

We've covered a lot of information in this book. The application of what you've learned will give you a massive competitive advantage in your marketplace and organisation. What follows is what I consider to be timeless advice. By applying it, along with the content of this book, you'll set yourself on course to be a leader in your field for the life of your career.

Emotional banking

When I became a sales manager, an experienced colleague of mine (let's call him Jon) taught me about the idea of an emotional bank account. I later learned that this principle is from *The 7 Habits of Highly Effective People*, by Stephen Covey.[20] The principle works the same way as a traditional bank account. To have a positive balance, you need to make deposits into the account. If you make too many withdrawals, you'll be overdrawn. Jon ensured that he provided his sales team with support, praise, reassurance and encouragement – all were deposits in their Emotional Bank Accounts. Sometimes he'd make short-notice requests of his team, which would constitute a withdrawal from their Emotional Bank Accounts, but he

---

20 S Covey, *The 7 Habits of Highly Effective People* (Simon and Schuster, 1989)

continually invested in his team so that the balance remained positive.

Keep this principle in mind to maintain a positive relationship with your clients. All the small deposits you make will positively impact your client – for example, doing what you say you'll do when you say you'll do it, sending them information you think they'll get value from, helping them with problems unrelated to your products or service, introducing them to other clients you think they'll like, etc. By investing in them this way, you'll also be able to make requests of your clients (but only when the balance of the 'account' is positive).

If you keep this principle in mind with your clients, they will move heaven and earth for you and your sales will take off.

Prioritise and execute

As the story at the start of this chapter showed us, not every account, client or sales opportunity is equal. It's critical to your success to identify your greatest opportunities and your priority accounts and clients. We all have accounts and clients that we know deep down aren't the best use of our time. Be honest with yourself, learn how to better prioritise your time and identify and minimise distractions. Getting clear on *where you will* invest your time and *where you will not* will be a game-changer.

You need to learn to say no to some clients, colleagues and even your manager. Once you're clear on your priority accounts, clients and opportunities, you must spend a disproportionate amount of time on them. Become laser focused on moving these opportunities forward and maximising your time serving these clients and accounts. The impact this will have on your time and your results might just astound you.

Keep your client at the heart of everything you do

Let this become your guiding principle in your sales career. The most important person to you as a salesperson is your client – nothing else matters as much. If your client has an issue, resolve it; if they have a need you can meet, fulfil it. If you truly have their best interests at heart, they will know it instinctively. You must get this into your unconscious mind. Set the intention to make satisfying your client your highest priority. Once you've done so, clients will be drawn to work with you, your meetings will be positive, your network will expand, opportunities will be created effortlessly and you won't have to concern yourself with client retention. A genuine focus on creating value for your clients will repay you over and over again. The desire to reciprocate value with commitment is a natural and powerful force in client–salesperson relationships.

Under-promise, over-deliver

I was taught this saying early in my sales career. My interpretation of it has served me well over the years: 'Promise, then over-deliver.' It's not about misleading your clients or misrepresenting the service your business can deliver – it's about being open, honest and not making promises you can't keep. When you're making commitments to your clients, or they're making requests of you and your business, you must be honest about what you can and cannot offer. Once you've made a commitment, you must honour it, or you risk damaging your credibility and that of your company. If you can, create additional value for your clients after a meeting. This is what it means to over-deliver. It's about making an extra effort to delight your client. It's about giving them something that they didn't expect, which will earn you appreciation and long-term loyalty. This is where the magic happens. The trust in your relationship solidifies and your career accelerates.

Gratitude: give and you shall receive

Whatever your beliefs, I encourage you to cultivate an 'attitude of gratitude'. When you're grateful, everything flows – your relationships get stronger, your outlook on life improves and your confidence grows. Focusing on what you have that you can be grateful for can be a humbling, rewarding practice that gives you a positive perspective on every part of your life. Your clients, colleagues, friends and loved ones will notice and feel even more connected and attracted to you.

If you can combine your attitude of gratitude with a genuine desire to create value for your clients, you'll build healthy, fulfilling relationships based on trust. You'll naturally demonstrate to your clients the confidence and support they need from you to choose you as their 'preferred partner', a position beyond salesperson.

Emotions are everything

In Chapter 7, we looked at how emotions are involved in buying decisions. Remember, your clients have a life outside of work. They have friends, family, hobbies, interests and passions. Learn what creates a fire inside your client, understand what makes their heart sing and find a way to genuinely connect with them on these topics. Being interested in your client and their life shows your respect and regard for them. Once you've established a common bond, you can build a relationship in which you and your client make decisions that are best for both of you.

Park your ego

You may work with clients who have an 'edginess' to them. In other words, a sense of superiority. In these situations, it can be easy to get drawn into disagreements. You've likely found yourself in meetings where you're desperate to correct your client or state your opinion after they've said something opinionated or blinkered. Unless you know them very well, or they're not an important client to you, simply be curious. If you can default to curiosity, you'll bypass your ego. This doesn't mean you should let clients walk all over you – you have values and principles that need to be respected. Rather, you should know when to remain calm and curious.

Revisit Chapter 11 and adopt the ritual of 'parking your ego' at the front door when you visit your clients. It will start to come naturally.

Selling and social media

A new world has opened up to salespeople through social media. It's become an influential channel through which you can identify, connect with and influence your clients. Research suggests that as many as 75% of buyers will use social media in their research of suppliers.[21] Used consistently and appropriately, social media can enhance and accelerate your sales cycle with your clients. You can use social media platforms to deliver countless types of content, including independent-expert reports/ findings, empowering quotations, challenging questions and positive client experiences, all of which will help you attract the attention of your current and future clients. Before you start creating content, cast a critical eye over your profiles:

- Make sure they're up to date, accurate and professional.

- Ensure they include only relevant and compelling information.

- Check for correct spelling, grammar and capitalisation.

- Identify a connection whose profile looks highly professional and ask for their feedback on your profiles.

This is important because clients will view your profiles before they connect with you. Consider what you want them to think when they view your profiles and make sure they will elicit that response. Remember too that clients will be notified of everything you like,

21 K Schaub, 'Social buying meets social selling: How trusted networks improve the purchase experience' [white paper] (IDC, 2014), https://business.linkedin.com/content/dam/business/sales-solutions/global/en_US/c/pdfs/idc-wp-247829.pdf, accessed 13 October 2020

comment on and share, so do so considerately and wisely.

Once you're satisfied with your profiles, there are a number of ways in which you can effectively make use of them. Here are some pointers:

- Decide on your top three social media objectives and use these as your guide when creating, posting and sharing content. For example:
  1. Increase my network of potential clients and influencers
  2. Build my credibility and personal brand/reputation
  3. Stimulate interest in my content and generate enquiries
- Follow experts in your field and comment on and share their content.
- When there's an issue in your marketplace, pose a question about it.
- Use hard data as a reference and/or to raise a challenge.
- Employ humour where possible – consider how your posts can make readers smile.
- Pose a question that isn't relevant to your business but is relevant to your clients.

- Review LinkedIn Groups and join those that are relevant to your clients.

- Post images, files and links to interesting sites and content.

- Challenge your organisation's marketing team to create a content plan for social media.

This list can serve as a starting point. The more engaged you are with social media, the more value you'll get from it.

It's easy to get distracted when using social media, so maintain your discipline when you log in. Develop the habit of logging in for a specific purpose – to meet your three objectives. Capture them in your journal or notebook under the heading *Social Media Objectives*.

When you use social media to create client value and generate enquiries, it's no longer a 'social' activity – it's fundamental to your sales process and you should think about it that way. I encourage you to consider carefully how you can integrate social media into your sales cycle and schedule regular time to act on your recommendations.

A double-edged sword

There are plenty of negative stories about social media out there, and I'm sure you've heard many. It's important to take great care when it comes to your social media profiles and posts. Also be mindful of where you're being tagged – if your profiles are public, the content linked to you on social media will be visible for all to see. Your profiles act as your shop window to the world, so make sure they're appealing and intentional.

A few years ago, a friend and business acquaintance told me about a role he and a colleague were recruiting for. Prior to interviewing the applicants, they reviewed their profiles on LinkedIn and Facebook to make sure that they matched the branding and image that the company wanted to project. He told me that a search of one applicant's Facebook profile turned up pictures of her dancing topless in a nightclub. She didn't receive an interview. Since hearing this story, I now make checking LinkedIn and Facebook profiles one of my first tasks when I'm dealing with a new supplier, client or staff member.

Don't leave it to chance – make sure your profiles are professional.

Ask for referrals

We've covered at length the importance of understanding your clients' needs and meeting them. We've looked at how to create value for them. We've agreed that we need to demonstrate trust, confidence and support to satisfy our clients and receive their loyalty and commitment. We've also spoken about asking your clients for feedback at the end of each meeting so you can understand how to better serve them in the future and find ways to continually improve. When you consistently take this approach and genuinely over-deliver, your clients will want to recommend you.

Direct requests for recommendations can make some people feel uncomfortable, but there are other ways you can go about it. I suggest asking your best clients for referrals first (prioritise). They'll be your biggest advocates. And whenever you receive a referral, show your gratitude. It's the greatest gift a client can give you. Here are a few ways to generate referrals:

- Use your first client referral as your example and tell other clients how grateful you are for it.

- Create a referral card or leaflet that you can leave with your clients to pass on.

- Write a referral script that you can insert into an email. Then ask if your clients would feel comfortable sending it on to people in their network or sharing it on social media.

- Where possible, consider referrals you can make to your clients to help them.

If you integrate client referrals into your sales process, you'll expand your client base and grow your business more quickly.

Be a lifelong learner

I think of lifelong learning as an attitude towards yourself, your capabilities and, ultimately, your potential in the world. If you acknowledge that you can do anything you set your mind to, and commit to lifelong learning, the path to achieving all of your goals will be laid out for you. There are millions of books in the world. Add to that the amount of information available on the internet – tutorials, videos, blogs, webinars, reports, theses and many, many other mediums – and we have access to almost any type of information we could possibly seek out.

The material is out there. You just need to commit to lifelong learning, decide what you want to study, schedule the right amount (and frequency) of time for it and then apply / practise what you've learned. It really is that simple, but it starts with your commitment.

This is a good time to revisit the goals you set in Chapter 2. Get clear on what you want and work towards it. With commitment and ongoing action, you will create the life you could only have dreamt of in the past. Once you've achieved your goals, you'll no doubt create new, more ambitious ones. Keep surprising yourself in terms of how much you can achieve. And remember to take time to reflect on how far you've come.

In the future, when you've achieved your goals and transformed your life, people may ask you how you managed to be so successful. Be generous with your advice and be curious about them – what they want and how you might help.

Identify a mentor

Throughout my career, I've had several informal and formal mentors, all of whom have had a dramatic effect on my career and my life. I've also acted as a mentor to many people within my own and other organisations. It's a truly rewarding experience to support others' growth and help them fulfil their potential. I highly recommend working with a mentor. Here are the steps to take:

- Carefully identify a mentor – someone who has the skills, position, experience or role you aspire to achieve.

- Decide what you want to get from and give to the mentoring relationship.

- Plan how you'll approach your potential mentor.

- Be clear on what you're asking for – the time commitment involved and what their responsibilities are.

- Be humble, grateful, confident and positive when you approach them.

Mentoring is such a positive experience for both parties that, in my experience, it's rare that someone will say no. They may say 'not right now', and that's fine. Ask them when the right time is and schedule a first meeting. Follow the Prepare2 INSPIRe process when preparing for that meeting. You'll then know exactly what you want to get from the meeting and how to be sure of a positive outcome.

If you find the right mentor, you'll have an advocate and adviser for life. This is incredibly beneficial for self-confidence and self-belief. You'll also receive a wealth of personal development from the process of identifying, approaching and planning for the mentoring meetings – and, of course, from the mentoring itself.

Control the temperature

I learned about this quotation and the analogy on a leadership training programme I attended years ago. I love this analogy. It's easy to get swept away by the tide of activity, emotions, relationships and general 'stuff' happening in our lives. We become reactive to our environments, like a thermometer. For example, we may attend meetings where a lot of people complain, including our clients, and end up getting sucked into this attitude and going along with the majority. But you'll know when reacting to the current environment isn't the right thing to do. In these situations, simply ask yourself, 'Do I want to be a thermostat or a thermometer?' Remember, a thermostat creates the temperature. You can create the tone or climate rather than react to it, like a thermometer.

You have the power to choose. Be a thermostat!

Enjoy The Journey

Finally, enjoy your time with clients, friends and family. This might seem like an odd statement in a sales manual, but the more you enjoy your life, the more your clients will come to like, respect and appreciate you, or even love spending time with you. We spend about half of our waking lives at work – it's half of the journey through life, so it's important to enjoy it.

This enjoyment is a choice, a perspective – it's within your control. You can choose to adopt a sunny disposition and enjoy your current work, or you can choose to move to a role that will bring you this enjoyment.

If you'd like to join the Focus4Growth sales community, you can connect with us at www.facebook.com/Focus4growth.

Thank you for reading this book. I wish you the greatest success possible.

I wish you happiness, health and joy.

Most of all, I wish you everything you wish for yourself.

Acknowledgements

Thank you to all the excellent salespeople I've worked with in the past, the sales trainers I've had the pleasure of training with and the challenging discussions we've had about what works in practice and what doesn't. Thank you to the best sales managers and coaches I've worked with (and the worst) – you can learn something from everyone: the good, the bad and the ugly. Thank you to my many clients and colleagues over the last twenty-five years, both those who supported me throughout my sales career and those who challenged me, didn't buy from me and made me reflect, learn, change and drive myself towards continuous improvement.

Thank you to the inspiring authors of the countless books I've had the pleasure of reading – books about NLP, psychology, success, business leadership, sales, coaching and performance. The application of this information has shaped and strengthened me throughout my career and my life, and thankfully the journey continues!

Thank you to my family for your never-ending belief in my abilities, my journey and the future destination. I know I've challenged the boundaries with my ideas, creativity and future vision, but what is life for if not to dream big?

The Author

Justin Leigh is the founder and managing director of Focus-4Growth Ltd. A business owner with over twenty-five years' experience in sales, strategic account management and business leadership, he has a track record of rapidly growing businesses across multiple market segments, including medical devices, dental products and services, IT accessories, OEM supply, industrial markets, and healthcare IT software.

An accredited executive coach, Justin is also an accomplished author, trainer, facilitator, adviser and consultant to board-level executives and teams. He works with clients and organisations across many sectors, including technology, insurance, dental, medical, FinTech, financial services, MedTech, media, business travel, security communications and business services.

Justin is passionate about helping people to grow, inspiring them to reach outstanding levels of performance through continuous improvement and clear, accountable action.

He is the author of a number of sales and business growth programmes, including:

- The RISE and Prepare2 INSPIRe Sales Training and Coaching Programme

- The Plan2 Coach Sales Leadership Programme

- Increasing Resilience, Accelerating Productivity

- The Leadership Acceleration Programme

Justin lives in Cambridgeshire, England, with his wife and two children.

Contact

If you would like to enquire about working with Justin and his team at Focus4Growth, you can contact them at:

in www.linkedin.com/in/business-sales-acceleration

f www.facebook.com/justin.leigh.71/about
www.facebook.com/groups/B2BSalesMastery

🌐 www.justin-leigh.com
www.focus4growth.co.uk
https://bit.ly/Sales-Mastery-Prog

📷 @focus4growth

♪ @oneminutecoach

Printed in Great Britain
by Amazon